Fed up *to* Start Up

**A STORY OF STRENGTH AND
THE VALUE OF YOUR CONNECTIONS**

TEQUILA PRESS

Sister Tequila Press
Contact: SisterTequilaPress@gmail.com

Most Sister Tequila Press books are available for special quantity discounts for bulk purchases for sales promotions, premiums, fund-raising and educational needs. Special books or excerpts also can be created to fit specific needs. For details write: SisterTequilaPress@gmail.com

ISBN # 978-0-578-61136-5 (paperback)
Library of Congress Control Number: 2023903847

Printed in the United States of America

Book design by Cassandra Voors

Fed up *to*
Start Up

**A STORY OF STRENGTH AND
THE VALUE OF YOUR CONNECTIONS**

Enjoy the ride!!

Robbie Hardy

ROBBIE HARDY

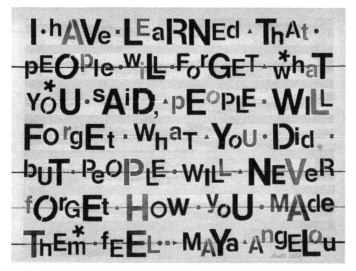

"

I've learned that people will forget what you said, people will forget what you did, but people will never forget how you made them feel.

—MAYA ANGELOU

This book is dedicated to all of my tribe, my community, my network, my connections. You are always there when I come calling, give me inspiration, push me to be smarter, make me question the whys and why nots (and make me wonder if I am crazy), but are always there for me in some shape or form. I cannot thank you enough for all you have done for me—it is truly priceless.

This book is also dedicated to all the founders out there; those thinking about making the move from the corporate world to the entrepreneurial world, those already there, and those dreaming about maybe someday starting their own company—this book is for you.

Table of Contents

Introduction

THE ENTREPRENEURIAL ROAD IS NOT easy and being a founder can be lonely at times. Perhaps you are already on the entrepreneurial road, or considering starting. Let me tell you; the high of building something from nothing with a team of amazing people is extraordinary. Coupled with the surge of validation when companies or businesses buy the product or service you create is hard to describe. It becomes addictive to be in this world of crazy ideas, successes, failures, investors and supportive families. They will wonder why it takes so much time to work for your self, shouldn't it be easier? Entrepreneurship is certainly not for the faint of heart.

My journey to entrepreneurship started as I sat in front of a Lego set, methodically clicking the bright plastic pieces into place. I never saw myself as an entrepreneur but rather a square peg in a round hole in the corporate consulting world. I was successful running teams and billing clients, but there always seemed to be something missing. I always volunteered to lead efforts that were remote from HQ, where I could create my own culture and sense of team. Looking up the corporate ladder, it became obvious that my teams and successes were a means to a promotion for the people above me. The constant shuffle of people in and out of positions, with the scope of work ever changing and the pressure to bill, bill, bill, was unrelenting.

It was so frustrating that I took up building Lego sets. I didn't know why at first. And as I meticulously followed the instructions, snapped the pieces into place, and celebrated each new page of the booklet, it dawned on me. I needed the satisfaction of seeing something completed. And I would never get that at my current job.

I left the corporate world and have never looked back.

My first company inspired this book. And when I say inspired, I do mean the Hollywood "inspired by true events" usage, where the story beats are the same, but the details have been entirely changed. We could say it is to protect the innocent, but I also moved the events to the present, where the advice is much more relevant. You see, all this transpired when there were even fewer women in the CEO seat and even fewer who invested in women like me. I had no idea at the time how unusual my successful technology startup was, with a woman *(gasp)* at the helm.

Thankfully things have changed, (at the time I just put my head down and worked) but none of that company's success would have happened without my network, my tribe, my village, my community, my connections. I reached out for help in so many ways, in so many places, and people were there for me, to make introductions to people, to explain crazy investment terms, to help me understand how to manage a board of directors and the list goes on and on. These connections were invaluable, and I did not even recognize how valuable until I was on the other side of this adventure.

Ultimately, that is what this book is about. The value of the people you know, worked with, went to school with, or had a bad glass of wine with at a conference, these are the people who will be there for you. They are the ones with the keys to your success. More importantly you need to be there for them; what goes around comes around. If you only take one thing from this book, let it be the priceless value of your tribe!

Fed-Up to Start-Up is the second in a three-book series, *Time to Rise*. The first book is *Upsetting the Table: Women Mentoring Women*, a story of climbing the corporate ladder and the value of mentoring. The third book is in the works. It is a story of upending the angel investment world, as a woman investing in women. You can read these books in any order, whatever speaks to you where you are in your journey.

All of these books are to help you on your way to success, however you define it. They aren't just about business, but about life. You aren't just a cog in a corporate machine or an entrepreneur in a bubble. Life happens at the same time, and these books include how messy it can be to navigate work and personal hurdles. Mostly, I want you to know that you can succeed. That the odds may be stacked and at some point it will be dark, and dawn will feel a long way off.

But you have what you need to succeed.

How do I know? Well, you've picked up this book. That shows curiosity and a willingness to learn. From there, all else will flow.

All my best,

Roslie Hardy

Chapter One

REBECCA STEPPED OUT OF THE skyscraper into the cool San Francisco air, buoyed by the outcome of the meeting she just nailed. She had secured an agreement that would boost her over her quarterly sales target and make quite a large dent in her annual target as well. Out on the street, she scanned expectantly down the bumper-to-bumper cars.

Her rideshare was supposedly just coming around the corner, but as she checked the status on her phone, the car suddenly was laterally transported three blocks south. Rebecca frowned at the tall buildings around her. You would think someone would have fixed GPS errors in downtown metroplexes by now.

Her phone buzzed.

LINDSEY THE BOSS LADY: *How did it go?*

> Good! I've already contacted legal to update the contract and send. Fingers crossed, I shouldn't need to come back until delivery (or later).

LINDSEY THE BOSS LADY: *You're still on the red eye, right?*

Typical Lindsey. No "nice job," no "way to pad that bottom line."

Rebecca flipped over to the rideshare app. The poor guy was crawling through traffic but should only be a few more minutes.

Rebecca flipped back to the text message from Lindsey, debating what to say. Technically, yes, she was booked on the red eye, but it stung. She managed a very profitable department in an international consulting firm, Regent Management Systems (RMS), and her department was always in the top ten revenue producers. She really resented having to "Lindsey watch" every penny to make up for those who didn't produce at the same level.

The cool air suddenly picked up speed as it whipped through the buildings, becoming cold and biting. She eyed the taxi stand across the street, considering jumping in just to get out of the wind, but no. This rideshare guy wasn't getting paid to sit in traffic on his way to pick her up. The least she could do was wait.

Her phone buzzed again.

TORI THE MAGNIFICENT OFFSPRING: *Who was supposed to pick me up from tennis?*

> *Dad*

TORI THE MAGNIFICENT OFFSPRING: *Ugh.*

> *Is there anyone there who can still give you a ride?*

TORI THE MAGNIFICENT OFFSPRING: *I already figured it out, Meghan's dad took me home.*

Rebecca glanced at the time and did the mental time zone calculation. It didn't add up. She swiped over to talk with Richard.

Are you waiting at the tennis courts?

RICHARD THE LOVE OF MY LIFE: *YES. Where is everybody?!*

Calendar mix up? Practice was moved an hour early (I think) Tori is already home – remind me to thank Meghan's dad later.

A GIF of a man banging his head against a steering wheel appeared on Rebecca's phone.

Love you, babe

A new alert chimed to her phone. Her ride was here.

Rebecca glanced up to see a sleek red Tesla waiting at the curb. A young man smiled expectantly behind the wheel. Rebecca felt a huge grin stretch across her face. Weather aside, she loved this town.

She opened the passenger door. "What's the deal with this fancy car?"

"I know, right?" replied the driver.

Rebecca hopped in eagerly. "Let's be clear. I usually don't jump in the front seat with strangers driving. But … You're doing rideshares in a 100K car."

"It's not mine."

Rebecca stopped mid-seatbelt pull and raised a teasing eyebrow at the driver. "Don't tell me you stole it, because I can get out right here."

"If I stole it, I would be heading south, enjoying ocean breezes for my last hour of freedom. Or fifteen minutes. This car is wired to the gills with anti-theft mojo."

Rebecca finished clicking her seatbelt in place. "Fair. But I'd go north to wine country."

"Is that where we're going?"

"I wish. But no, we're headed to the airport." Rebecca ran her hands over the seat and eyed the digital center dashboard. *Geez, this is a nice car.*

"Ah. Well, I'm supposed to encourage you to press all the buttons, enjoy the reclining seats, and basically do anything you want except drive the car yourself."

"Is this a sales gimmick?"

"Basically, yeah. There's some sort of tech convention happening in town this week. Deep pockets, love of technology, Tesla's prime audience. They loaned the fleet a bunch of their cars through Sunday. I'm going to be so sad to turn it back in."

Rebecca hardly heard him as she tapped through all the options in the digital dashboard. "Oh, can we do the autopilot?"

The driver laughed. "Everyone wants to try that. It's like they don't trust my driving."

Rebecca laughed too. A vibration in her pocket brought her back to reality. The unanswered text message now had a follow up.

Lindsey The Boss Lady: *You're still on the red eye, right?*

Lindsey The Boss Lady: *The 8am meeting tomorrow is mandatory.*

Rebecca scrunched up her face in displeasure. But if she was ever going to afford a car like this, she had to play ball.

I'll be there.

"Who was that?"

Rebecca glanced over at the driver.

"Sorry, none of my business. It's just that your whole energy changed there."

"Did it?" she queried.

He nodded.

"It's my by-the-numbers boss, being by-the-numbers."

"She's a vibe killer, for sure," the driver replied.

"Ruining your driving energy?"

"Definitely. But you know what will get our mojo back? Figuring out the radio and playing some sweet tunes."

Rebecca used her computer science degree to find the radio options and adjust the station. "You've got to love it. This is so San Francisco. A rideshare in a hundred-thousand-dollar car that can drive itself, and your driver is an energy healer when the autopilot is turned on."

The driver laughed. "Are you saying I should turn the autopilot off and stick to driving?"

"Nope. You keep being you. This is great."

Another vibration.

Travis – Airport Squad: *You almost here?*

A picture of a neatly made Manhattan appeared on her screen.

The driver turned towards her briefly. "Whoever that is…that's good energy right there."

———

Rebecca was still smiling when she made it through security at San Francisco International Airport. The driver, whose name turned out to be Xavier, had made a solemn pinkie swear with her before dropping her off: they would both one day own a car like this. It was like pinkie swearing they would both be astronauts on the moon, but still a lot of fun to think about.

TRAVIS—AIRPORT SQUAD: *I'm going to drink your drink if you're not here in the next 30 seconds.*

Don't lie. You know you ordered it for yourself.

TRAVIS—AIRPORT SQUAD: *I admit nothing. Seriously tho, Jeremy has big news and is crawling the walls with excitement for everyone to get here. I might kill him if he says "where's Rebecca" one more time.*

Rebecca laughed to herself as she waltzed into the Frequent Flyer lounge.

And there, taking over three tables and gleefully annoying the solo drinkers, was her "airport squad."

"There she is." Travis sauntered over with a drink in-hand.

"Oh, did I make it in thirty seconds? Good. I had to wind sprint at the end, totally took out a family of four. Knocked them over like bowling pins."

"Yes …" He handed over the glass. "You should go back out there and tell them that their sacrifices were well worth it."

Rebecca sipped her drink tentatively. The extra cold, sweet yet bitter complexity of flavors was just what she needed.

Travis raised an eyebrow.

"Perfect," she confirmed his unasked question. "What's this news we're all here for?"

Travis, ever the gentleman, grabbed her rolling suitcase and escorted her to the gathering. "No idea, but Sarah and Jacob aren't here yet, so help me distract him."

The airport squad had started as a loose coalition of co-workers flying in and out of cities and connecting in the airport lounge for a quick pre-meeting before heading over to their large corporate clients. It quickly expanded to include colleagues and executives from other companies working on the same projects. As people moved companies and were promoted, the squad grew to include a revolving circle of brilliant businesspeople. It was a lucky group of people that she got to work with and liked being around. They understood each other and all the idiosyncrasies of their clients and the endless travel.

Jeremy, as usual, was holding court at the center table, cracking jokes, and talking with his hands so enthusiastically that the drinks were in danger of being toppled. He stood when he spotted Rebecca. "I'm so glad you made it! What took so long? Did you land a deal to sell a million licenses, your first child, and your soul?"

"My first child, for sure. Not quite a million licenses, but if you count all the little ones and zeros, I'm sure there's a cool trillion in there. And I'd sell my soul to have the car I got picked up in for my rideshare. Guess what it was."

The whole group was suitably impressed by Rebecca's retelling of her top of the line rideshare and the energy healing driver. The squad agreed that the driver was right, that they were good energy.

"I just wish I could buy one. It's a million times more than I've ever spent on a car."

"It's decadent," Travis agreed, "but I'd do it."

A few others chimed in, and soon there was a vote and a raise of hands at the table.

Jeremy then jumped in and said, "Hmm. I can't wait anymore. I have to share my news now." He pattered his fingers on the table, creating his own drumroll. "My big news is … that I quit my job!" He watched them all, with clear excitement.

"Congrats. Which company are you going to?" Travis asked.

"Not company. Country. Bali first. Then maybe the Philippines? After that, wherever my feet take me."

"Wait, what?" Rebecca wasn't sure she was hearing this right. Jeremy had always been the center of any party, but his work was always rock solid. She couldn't fathom why he would run off to parts unknown. She looked around at the equally blank faces of the squad.

"I quit. Well, first I saved – then I quit. And I'm going to sell basically everything when I get back to Dallas. I've got two weeks left, then I'm headed out for the territories."

There was silence at the table. It was awkward, like someone announcing to the pub regulars that he was headed to AA in the morning.

Rebecca briefly entertained the idea. If money and responsibilities disappeared, what would she do? And the answer was a complete blank space, a weirdly yawning void of nothing. "What will you do?" Rebecca finally blurted.

"Have an adventure? Make memories? Enjoy not working seven days a week for a boss and a company who wouldn't notice if I died?"

"Oh, yeah," Travis supplied. "Anthony in legal died, and they just moved the pile of work to the next desk over and that was it."

"Exactly." Jeremy gestured around him. "I got up every morning to go to work, to buy things and pay for a place to keep those things. And then one day I woke up and just had this moment of: what am I doing with my life? I don't like my job, and I don't really like my things. What am I doing?"

"Wow." Rebecca could feel her eyebrows furrowing. She just couldn't fathom walking away from her responsibilities like that. But she was genuinely happy for him. "Congrats, Jeremy. I hope you're really happy. Let me buy you a drink to celebrate."

"Not on your life, Rebecca." Jeremy grinned at her. "Manhattans taste like fruity cough syrup. But you can definitely buy me a cosmo."

———

Rebecca spent the majority of the five-hour flight home working, catching dirty looks from passengers bothered by the light from her laptop, and berating herself for not being able to just sleep. Try as she might, she had never been one to sleep on a plane. Sleeping pills seemed to only take effect the moment she got off the plane. That wouldn't be so bad if she had a bed to fall into and could get some shut eye before the day started again, but she had to be sharp for whatever this "mandatory" meeting was first thing the next morning.

Lindsey was a penny-pincher and lived by spreadsheets, but she had been 'Extra Lindsey' this week, with a million reminders both by email and text and even a few calls. *What could be going on to warrant all this intensity*, Rebecca pondered. She hadn't had much time to think about it until she left the airport squad and now it was all she could think about.

Rebecca reviewed spreadsheet after spreadsheet of numbers for the umpteenth time. Her team was on track, if not a little ahead of her already aggressive plan. And as far as she knew, the other people called to this meeting were hitting their deliverables as well. It made her uneasy. She hadn't been kidding when she told Xavier that her boss was "by-the-numbers." Lindsey's name in her cellphone should be "Lindsey, By-The-Numbers." And in all these reports, Rebecca couldn't find a number out of place that would trigger a meeting like this.

By the time the cabin lights were unceremoniously flipped back on, Rebecca felt bone tired, and her eyes had acquired that sandpaper feeling.

This was going to be a long day.

———

At home, Richard was already up, drinking his morning coffee and scrolling through the news. Rebecca eyed the pile of dishes in the sink and decided she was too tired to say anything now. The dishes could stay in the sink forever, she wasn't touching them, but she wasn't above a stern discussion and a pointed jibe or two – once she had a shower, and maybe a nap.

"Have a good flight?" Richard asked.

Rebecca made a face. "I feel gross. I'm going to go clean up."

"I'll make you breakfast."

"I'll settle for your cup of coffee now."

Richard looked guiltily at his cup. "Recently vacated. I'll make a new one and bring it up."

"Deal."

True to his word, a few minutes later, Richard reached into the running shower with a steaming cup of hot coffee. Rebecca laughed with surprise. She cupped the mug in two hands and navigated sipping without getting shower water inside. "I take it all back. You really are the best."

Richard's voice floated from the other side of the shower door. "That's my job. To be the very best coffee delivery service in town."

"What happened while I was gone? You and Tori have a good time?"

There was an audible sigh on the other side of the door. Rebecca waited and sipped her cup. When a reply wasn't forthcoming, she prompted. "You want to talk about it?"

"Yeah, but I know you're tired. And I've got to get ready for my trip."

"Oh, that's right." Rebecca sighed. "Chicago?"

"And then New York. Maybe we could have a call tonight?"

Rebecca closed her eyes and briefly wished that they could both stay still, not be flying in different directions all the time. Richard had once asked her, after Tori was born, if she wanted to be a stay-at-home mom. He offered to be the breadwinner and create that 1950s sitcom household of lore. And even with that tiny baby in her arms and a million maternal hormones telling her to "say yes," the answer had been an emphatic "no." She wanted an equal marriage with both of them to share the money making, the child rearing, the household chores. She couldn't imagine being *that* woman who was just waiting for her husband to get home to make her whole.

Richard hadn't been surprised by her choice, and while their flourishing careers occasionally clashed with the care of their daughter, he hadn't brought it up again. She had always been fiercely independent, and he knew that from the start. She hadn't even taken his name when they got married.

"Sure, let's have a call. Here." She handed the cup back out of the shower. "For safe keeping – not drinking, Richard Daly."

"I solemnly swear to protect this cup with my life. Or to just leave it on the counter by your towel."

"Good man."

———

Downstairs, Rebecca set the bacon going and started slicing up a cantaloupe on the counter that was starting to smell ripe. If she timed it right, she could eat sitting down before she had to take Tori to school.

Speaking of the angel, Tori breezed into the kitchen. She stopped short and eyed the sizzling pan of bacon. "I know what you're doing, Mom. And that isn't fair."

Rebecca glanced up from the cantaloupe. "Trying not to slice off my fingers?"

"Dad told you I don't eat meat anymore and so you run out and start frying up the little piggies to tempt me back to the dark side."

Rebecca stared at Tori. "What do you mean, you don't eat meat anymore? We eat meat all the time."

"No, I don't."

"When I left on a plane two days ago, you did."

"Well, maybe if you were here, you'd know. I don't. Eat. Meat."

Rebecca stared at her daughter for a moment and then shrugged. "Take some cantaloupe then. I think there are some pecans in the pantry. You'll need something more to sustain you through to lunch time."

Tori eyed her mom for a moment, clearly wary of some sort of trap. When one wasn't forthcoming, she grabbed a bowl and scooped some cantaloupe into it. "That's it? You're not going to try to talk me out of it?"

"Nope. Your body, your choice. We'll have the veggie burritos you like, for dinner. But Dad and I are going to keep eating meat."

"Do you know where your meat comes from?"

"Animals, Tori. Meat comes from animals." Internally, Rebecca cringed. She didn't like the impatience in her voice. Even if her daughter was being an apex teenager.

"With faces. There is this giant pig that is part of this family in the Midwest, and it likes belly rubs, Mom. And there are millions of pigs just like it in factories all over the world that are penned up and forced to breed and never feel sunlight on their skin, and ..."

Richard breezed into the kitchen. "Oh, is it that pet pig again?" Richard fished a sizzling piece of bacon from the skillet and took a scalding bite. "He's delicious."

———

Rebecca rolled into the office at 7:45 A.M. and headed straight to the coffee pot in the second-floor break room. The weird silence in the car as she drove Tori to school was out of character and made Rebecca uneasy. They usually sang to music or talked about classes or friends. Tori seemed to be mad at her because she didn't give her any grief over her overnight vegetarianism. It boggled the mind that Tori was giving her the silent treatment for supporting her. Parenting a teenager was exhausting. Rebecca idly thought about investing in coffee to get her through the next three years until Tori left for college.

Richard wasn't helping either. His boy humor was funny to him, but it was putting Tori on the defensive. And frankly, it was gross too. She'd have to talk with Richard and come up with some brilliant way of saying: "don't be you right now."

Valarie strolled in as Rebecca worshipped her coffee mug.

"Ugh. I had to park all the way down in the 5th Street lot. I hate that place," she complained.

"That place is nasty." Rebecca glanced at her watch. "It's early for that too. I wonder if there's another big meeting going on somewhere."

"Not here." Valarie gave her nose a tap. "All the major department teams have hush-hush meetings this morning, but the worker bees are on their normal schedule."

Rebecca chewed this new piece of information over. There was shake-up coming. Maybe a reorganizing of the command structure. Part of her hoped that she would get to spin off with her team to tackle another business sector outside the sphere of Lindsey. Rebecca always loved a new challenge, but part of her knew it would be hard to give up all she had built.

Lindsey's cadre of direct reports were all women. It was super-rare in consulting firms, and Rebecca felt guilty that she wasn't enjoying it more. But all the women on the team (herself included) had climbed the corporate ladder in a man's industry to get to where they were now. And sometimes that meant that they clashed, were abrasive, were self-trained to push the limits prove themselves, and occasionally (purposely or inadvertently) kneecap each other in the process. They each acted like there was only one seat for a woman at any corporate table and they were determined to be in that chair.

It wasn't toxic, per se. More like a group of Olympic sprinters, best in their field, pushing each other to be the best when the game was on, and trash talking each other in the press before and after the match. They were all representing their own country of "Me", and Lindsey had failed to fold them into an Olympic Team.

That said, they were all driving each other to succeed through sheer competition. And the results were there. Lindsey had all the numbers to show them in every weekly meeting they had. Spreadsheet upon spreadsheet of numbers, their division was doing well.

"You ready for this?" Valarie interrupted Rebecca's train of thought.

"Any inside track on what it's all about?" Rebecca asked.

"Nope. But whatever it is, I'm sure we've seen worse."

Rebecca shrugged. Her career had mostly been unscathed by the housing crash of 2008, and the biggest struggle of working from home during the pandemic had been managing to juggle a bored child and a restless husband. She hadn't realized Richard was a stand and pace guy in the workplace, but on reflection, it did make sense. He was a medical sales rep, used to standing for hours on end in the operating room while talking to the doctors about the equipment they were using. Understanding hadn't made him any easier to quarantine with though.

Rebecca and Valarie headed down to the schedule board and found they were booked into the fourth-floor conference room. *Another ominous sign*, Rebecca thought. A conference room with frosted privacy windows. A quick glance through the rest of the board showed that the conference room and its identical siblings were booked through the rest of the morning, while the less secure conference rooms sat empty.

A pit formed in her stomach.

Valarie seemed completely unconcerned as they waited at the elevator bank, making idle chitchat. Rebecca knew Valarie wasn't clueless, but maybe she had reasons to be unconcerned.

Everyone except Lindsey was already in the conference room when they arrived. Cathy was in her accustomed seat nearest the head of the table. Teresa, who clashed with Cathy, had claimed the seat furthest from Cathy. This suited Rebecca just fine; she was too tired to deal with their fireworks.

"Have either of you seen Lindsey today? She's usually early to these things, not late," Teresa asked before the rest of the women could finish taking their seats.

Cathy sighed. "I already told you, she's hunkered in her office. She's been in there all morning."

"Well, someone might know more."

"I know nothing," Rebecca announced. "I just got in."

Valarie shrugged. "She'll get here when she gets here."

There was silence for a moment.

"I had to fly in this morning for whatever this is," Teresa ventured.

"Do you remember the last time we all got called in for some big brouhaha?" Cathy asked with a definitive tone. "It was to announce the company's new emerging markets plan. Everyone got reorganized, and then six months later, they scrapped it, and everyone went back to the old structure. Just you watch, it will be another soon-to-fail scheme."

Rebecca had to admire Cathy's bravado. She obviously had no better idea of what was going on and was charging confidently ahead like a brave little soldier. She was a company girl, through and through. Rebecca wondered briefly when she had lost that feeling of company loyalty.

After a few more minutes of Teresa and Cathy plucking at each other's nerves (and Valarie raising a conspiratorial "can you believe these two?" eyebrow in her direction), Lindsey finally graced them with her presence.

Or at least, the door opened, and her usual cart filled with a tall stack of binders slid themselves into the room.

Rebecca wondered how she was able to navigate the cart to the table without running smack into it.

At the last moment, Lindsey's perfectly coifed head popped out to the side of the stack and deftly maneuvered the cart, parking it neatly within arm's reach of the head of the table.

Rebecca watched with trepidation as Lindsey arranged the binders at the end of the table. Every spreadsheet in the department was undoubtedly three-hole punched and encased into one of these binders. Lindsey's major flaw as a leader was her by-the-numbers nature. The fact that she felt it necessary to bring all the numbers wasn't a reassuring sight.

There was some small talk as Lindsey settled in.

Rebecca felt like Lindsey was stalling, and finally everyone was silent, looking at her expectantly. The silence drew out.

Lindsey looked down at the reports in front of her, addressing them rather than the team. "Our department has done exemplary work the last two quarters. However, I've been informed that due to some missed opportunities and cancelled contracts in other departments, we need to reduce expenses, which of course means we're laying off some staff."

In the shocked silence, Rebecca picked up her pen and jotted down a question so she wouldn't forget it.

"How many staff?" Teresa asked tentatively.

"All of the major departments are being asked to make cuts." Lindsey dodged.

Valarie and Cathy demanded simultaneously – "How many people?"; "Do we still have jobs?" – their questions overlapping.

Rebecca sat quietly waiting for the details. *If one of them gets cut, there might be a new challenge to tackle. That could be fun.*

"You all still have jobs," Lindsey assured them, looking up from her spreadsheets for the first time. "But we're cutting twenty-five percent of the department." Her eyes had drifted back to the table, as if she couldn't believe the numbers had betrayed her.

"Who?" Teresa asked. "Is it already decided? Or ..." She glanced around the table. "Do *we* have to decide?"

"I've selected the least valuable team members." Lindsey gestured to the binders. "It's impartial, based solely on the performance and productivity matrix."

Rebecca felt like she was at a funeral and the person in the casket didn't know it yet. "This doesn't make any sense – you can't make layoff decisions based on the profitability of the individual. The best team members make broader contributions to the department, which leads to the end product, which drives sales and profitability."

"Exactly," Valarie chimed in. "Plus, you shouldn't be making any layoff decisions at all. *We* should be making the decisions, as we know the people and their value. And we have the P&L responsibility, so we need the authority too."

"Oh, you want to make emotional decisions then. Ones that will leave us open to lawsuits?"

"That is such a load of BS—"

"Lindsey, I'm not doing this."

Every head turned toward Rebecca.

"Give me the dollar amount I need to cut, and I'll give you a plan by close of business today, but first I'm going upstairs to have a conversation about how wrong this is."

And no one was more surprised than Rebecca, when she stood up and let her feet carry her out the door. It was only later that she had time to ponder the question she had written down: *What's my severance package?*

Chapter Two

CATHY, VALARIE, AND TERESA CAUGHT up to Rebecca at the elevator banks. When the doors slid open, they boarded as one and Rebecca hit the button for the top floor. Very little was said as they ascended the building. Over many years, Rebecca had learned that prepared speeches were useless in the heat of the moment, but if she could just hold the shape of the thing loosely in her head, it would come out just fine.

The shape of the thing in her head was indignation, betrayal, and a quiet little voice who knew things had been going too well – she should have known better.

The top floor and the lobby had a lot in common. It was all polished marble floors and plush furniture meant to impress the VIPs. In light of what was going on downstairs, it looked like a thin veneer, easily cracked.

The executive assistant looked up pleasantly from her computer and addressed them all.

Rebecca asked to speak to the COO.

The assistant was sorry; he wasn't there.

Rebecca asked to speak to the CFO.

He also wasn't in.

Rebecca rolled the dice and named the CEO of the company.

He too was not in.

She shoved down her frustration and smiled. "I'm oh-for-three. Is there an off-site meeting going on?"

The assistant bit her lip. "Yes," she admitted, clearly reluctantly.

Rebecca felt like there was more to the story. *Are they off somewhere trying to figure out how to get out of the layoffs?*

Cathy stepped forward. "Would this meeting happen to involve polo shirts and golf clubs?"

The assistant glanced around, seemingly to confirm they were alone, and then nodded.

Ahhhh. Rebecca felt a new feeling bubbling in her head – rage.

———

Downstairs in the lobby, Valarie declared the executive floor incapable of managing their tiny, tiny golf balls. It wasn't a particularly great joke, but it broke the tension. Suddenly, they were all chuckling, then outright laughing, in one of those contagious moments that they all desperately needed.

The four of them wandered down to an early lunch and to commiserate over appetizers.

Much to Rebecca's chagrin, Teresa had taken pity on Lindsey and invited her down too. Logically, she knew the situation wasn't Lindsey's fault, but the ridiculous methodology and by-the-numbers decisions she had made about Rebecca's team, without consulting her at all, had compounded a bad situation and made it worse.

No, Rebecca reminded herself. *The fault falls to the club-swinging boys on the top floor who are so far removed from the consequences of their decisions that they can't be bothered to be in the building as they tank their revenue. And then when they realize what they did next quarter when they didn't get their bonuses, they'll be outraged and make some other terrible choices.*

That bothered Rebecca more than the layoffs. How could she ever feel secure in her own career after this? Her best programmers did more than just code. They spent time confirming the requirements, conferring with the customers, and figuring out how to lift the whole team. Those contributions weren't quantified in a spreadsheet. And now they were basically sending her most essential team members in a limo to their competitors. So next quarter when profits were down, would it be her job next?

"Lindsey, are you sure it's got to be twenty-five percent?" Rebecca asked as soon as the thought had formed in her head.

"I was told twenty-five percent."

"But if the company could save those salaries some other way, we could keep them? Or at least some of them?"

"Maybe?" Lindsey guessed. "They may have tightened the belt already though; I really don't know. I didn't ask."

Typical, Rebecca thought.

Rebecca was even more frustrated that Lindsey just took the number without fully understanding it. She was a VP, but she was so busy playing with the numbers you would never know it. Rebecca wondered how they had come to decide that twenty-five percent cuts of some unknown number of departments would solve their problems. If she could find other, more strategic places to cut, maybe there was a chance.

The rest of lunch became a brainstorm of wasteful expenditures, with a sizeable list of possibilities at the end.

Rebecca left lunch feeling a little more hopeful than she had when she walked in.

The phone call with Richard that night was hard. She wished he was home so that he could give her a hug. And if he could see her face when he asked questions, he would know that he was giving her a panic attack, not comfort.

According to Richard, if the company was laying off more than ten percent of the workforce, they had to give advance warning or they could be sued. Rebecca tried to do the calculation based on the departments she had been told, but without a current employee count, or real numbers for the other departments, it was a case of unproductive guesswork. And then she chastised herself for being worried about the company. It was the *employees* she needed to care about.

Finally, she admitted to Richard what she'd written on the notepad. "If I had been fired, I had my one and only question right there. What is my severance package? I would have walked out right then and gone to a movie. This feels so much worse. I still have a job that will be impossible to do without my staff. I'm not going to be able to produce at the level I am now, and I'll have to watch my competitors kick my ass. Because you know they're going to be hiring some of my best people – plus, how many others are going to walk out the door with them? All that talent is going to cross the street to a competitor, and a year from now, we'll be way behind and—"

"I'm sorry, honey." Richard stepped in, to obviously head off the coming panic attack. "But out of curiosity, which movie?"

Rebecca felt the corner of her mouth turn up. "Something with lots of guns and explosions. You know, the stupid ones you love."

"Ah, I had you pegged for a superhero movie. You know, the ones with colorful spandex and quippy one liners."

"Hm. I think Spiderman 24 is in theaters now. Or maybe it was James Bond 87. Something like that."

"You want to come up here and we can go to one of those cheesy musicals you love?"

"As much as I would love to, I've got to meet with legal tomorrow, and I have that flight to Florida to meet those clients ... you remember them."

"The country club snobs? I remember them. If they ask, the 19th hole at our golf course has the old-school Disneyland ticket system. E-tickets get you Coors."

"A-tickets get you the hard stuff?"

"I wouldn't know," Richard joked. "My wife only leaves me the E-tickets."

"She sounds like a terrible woman."

"She is, she breaks my heart every day. Do you want to come rescue me from my loveless marriage?"

"Yes, I will go kick her out of the bed right now."

"You're a good woman, Rebecca Hoffman."

"I love you."

"Love you too."

Rebecca sighed and put the phone away. The flirting was nice, but if Richard had been in the room, he may have realized she still needed to talk it out rather than change the subject. With them both traveling like this, so many times, she just surrendered to the abrupt change in conversation. It was easier that way, but it left her feeling a little unheard. However, the call had worked in its own way, making her step back and look at the problem with some distance. And maybe, just maybe, she'd find an alternative solution to letting her team members go.

———

The meeting with the legal department was fraught with tension for Rebecca. They worked together preparing all the emotionless paperwork to hand to people who were about to be unemployed through no fault of their own. The two corporate lawyers and Rebecca had gone over the compensation numbers for each employee, verified the individual packets, and then the two lawyers had topped the whole thing off by admonishing her in the right and wrong way to lay someone off. Apparently, Rebecca was to remain emotionless, not admit any responsibility, and not do or say anything that might come back to bite the company in a lawsuit.

It was nerve-wracking knowing what she had to do.

On the Florida trip, the clients did suggest dinner at a country club, and Rebecca gently pumped her counterparts for potential job openings. She wasn't legally allowed to say that RMS was going to do some layoffs, and while she was fumbling for the right words, she was worried they now thought she needed the job. It became a bit of a mess after that.

Finally, in the hotel room that night, Rebecca got to sit down with her spreadsheet and calculator. From her meeting with legal, she had a clear idea of what the average pay was in the department. She also had a list of possible over expenditures within the company and ideas for cutting costs.

Working well into the night, Rebecca scratched off some of the excess costs, but it wasn't enough to be able to save jobs. So, she flipped the equation, concentrating on what would make these jobs invaluable to the company. If she could show how these jobs could be a profit center ...

That night, Rebecca roughly sketched out a persistent problem in the marketplace and how her team could fill that gap. The market information was fairly straight-forward, since she'd been in this industry for years. The problem was a snarly one that took several drafts to describe. Then she drafted (and redrafted) the solution, taking it from bullet points to an in-depth process.

The next step was a little fuzzy. On the flight back from Florida, Rebecca considered her options. If she asked for a meeting to present her plan, it likely would be a "no" straight away. They didn't understand the real value of her proposal, as they were too far removed from the day to day, so why would they take the meeting? If they did take the meeting, they likely wouldn't be prepared to say "yes" in the room, and to save jobs, she needed them to take the leap.

Finally, she decided to send the meeting request with a cover email explaining enough of the project to get the VPs to open the attached report. She also CC'd Lindsey, so it was apparent that she wasn't going above anyone's head or wasn't above board. That kind of behavior would also get her an instant "no."

And now here she was, nervous butterflies pounding at her belly as she and Lindsey rode the elevator to the executive floor. Rebecca didn't normally get nervous when she stuck her neck out, but as she ran through possible outcomes, it did occur to her that they were already axing jobs, so she may have inadvertently put her career in the guillotine too.

Twenty minutes later, Rebecca was unceremoniously returning to her own floor.

Her presentation had been cut off almost as soon as it started. The VP saw the need for a product to fill the problem she found, and he thanked her for the extra effort. However, he wouldn't consider exploring the issue until the third quarter of next year.

Why? *Because doing his job might interfere with his tee time,* Rebecca thought bitterly.

She held the rejected report in her hand. Really, it wasn't that complicated of a product. It was just another stream of income.

Anyone could do it.

The elevator dinged as it arrived on her floor.

Rebecca went to her office and shut the door. She flipped through the report again, this time looking for hiccups, flaws, anything that would make this product proprietary to the company. Could any other company really come up with this solution?

The answer, Rebecca decided, was no. Her company was the only one who could create this product because she was an employee when she proposed the idea.

That was it. The company had brand recognition and relationships, but the stream of income could actually be developed by any company. This particular idea, however, belonged to the company because she had been their employee, used their resources, and presented it to the company with their logo on the presentation.

This idea was dead for third-party development, but suddenly the wheels were turning.

If she could come up with one idea, in one night, and flesh it out and get it in front of decision makers in less than forty-eight hours, what could she do if she was the decision maker?

What other problems are out there looking for solutions?

Rebecca stared at the office walls. Was she really considering leaving this?

Yes. For the right idea, absolutely.

Rebecca broke out her cell phone and thumbed to the Airport Squad group chat. There was already a meet-up being arranged for DFW in two weeks. She RSVP'd and dropped a hint that she had big stuff to discuss with the group. For confidentiality rules, she might not be able to bring this idea to the group, but she could approach the group with other ideas, or they might have problems they see that could use a third-party solution.

As she left work that day, Rebecca felt better than she had all week.

Chapter Three

REBECCA'S FLIGHT WAS TWENTY MINUTES late to DFW and still she was the first one to make it to the designated lounge. There had been a cold front sweeping down from the north, snarling all the air traffic out of Chicago. She hoped that the others would be able to make it. They had all caught flights with the intention of meeting in the evening and then proceeding to their various clients in and around downtown Dallas tomorrow morning. Now, the weather had its own plans.

She chuckled to herself as she got settled in to wait. Every one of her Airport Squad was a frequent flyer and had their strong opinions about the VIP club privileges their corporate travel cards bought them. They each had a favorite lounge in their favorite terminal, for each airport where they traveled. And she had been so excited to meet with them, Rebecca had just blindly agreed as they decided the meet-up. And now here she was, in her least favorite lounge, in her least favorite terminal, hunkering down for the long haul. She hoped someone would get there soon to distract her from her butterflies.

Butterflies, again. It was previously unimaginable being so nervous, but perhaps it was an indicator of how much she cared about her new ideas. She opened her laptop and pulled up a familiar spreadsheet. This Airport Squad was her safe place, where she could relax. She scanned the list in the "A" column.

No, she wasn't nervous to share the list with them. She was nervous about what she'd do next.

She had spent the last two weeks brainstorming, fleshing ideas out, and discarding them. Then one night, she had read a bunch of articles on being an entrepreneur, watched numerous Ted Talks with conflicting advice to the articles, then fell asleep watching videos of pets greeting their soldiers.

The next morning, she had decided that at least some of the ideas had merit and deserved a presentation. So, she was about to present her short list of possible company ideas, ask for their opinions, and after that …

What if they thought her ideas were good? What then? Would she take the leap? Quit her job?

She was flipping through one of the ideas, idly filling in gaps when Travis slid into the seat across from her.

"That flight was rough. I got the turbulence, the crying baby, AND the lady who throws her hair over the back of the seat. She's lucky they confiscate the scissors at sec—"

Rebecca protectively snapped her laptop closed.

"What was that?" Travis guffawed. "You shut that down like a teenage boy caught looking at something naughty."

"Teenagers do that?" Rebecca replied innocently. "Close excel sheets when their friends come by?"

Travis eyed her, obviously amused. "Yes, they're known for their sneaky excel habits. Very daring with data management."

"I wouldn't know. Tori is obsessed with tennis and shopping. I know the boys and their *spreadsheets* are coming, but they aren't knocking on the door just yet."

"Wow." Travis snorted. "I don't think I'll be able to say that word again without blushing."

"You're welcome."

There was a silence as Travis looked pointedly at her and then the laptop, but Rebecca wasn't quite ready to share yet. And if she told Travis, she'd have to start over when the next person arrived, and so on until she was hoarse, and everyone was bored.

"I'll tell you when everyone gets here," Rebecca said. "Let me buy you a drink in the meantime."

"You drive a hard bargain."

———

An hour later, the Airport Squad had reached a quorum, and Rebecca was feeling deliciously comfortable after nursing a Manhattan. The butterflies had settled and when there was a lull in the conversation, Rebecca cleared her throat.

"So, I have ..." she hesitated "... not a presentation, or an announcement. Well, two weeks ago, I had to look a quarter of my staff in the eye and tell them they didn't have a job anymore. It was awful. And senseless. I've let people go before for poor performance; we all have ..."

There were some nods around the table.

"But this wasn't poor performance – it was because another division made a bad bet. And yes, bad bets have happened to most of us, but to make it really painful, the criteria for the layoffs was based on the employee's profitability, not performance. It was totally insane, illogical, and …" She took a deep breath. "It was the last straw for me."

It was the first time she'd said it out loud to anyone other than Richard. When no one gasped and a clap of lightning didn't shake the building, she felt it was okay to continue. "I tried to argue reason, and I even came up with this whole plan for a new business direction for the company, and it got shot down before I barely got it out of my mouth. I almost stormed out, Jerry Maguire style, but without a plan that would have been career suicide. So…"

"Is this the laptop part?" Travis piped up.

"Yes, sort of." Rebecca smiled. "I've spent the last two weeks trying to come up with problems that need solving. Things that can be solved by developing a product rather than the custom software solutions I manage now. I want something with leverage, build it once and sell it over and over." She then amended, "Because I can't fix the global warming problem or create world peace. But I'm looking at going independent, and I need a business that fixes a real problem and leverages the same contacts I've already got relationships with."

Rebecca could tell that she had lost the group a little there at the end. There were some confused looks when she had described solving problems. She opened the laptop and shared some of the ideas on her list to prime the pump.

"Oh, you want to know where the gaps are, so you can create a company to fill them? I get it. I hate it when I have to document client interactions in two different CRMs. Like, why can't it port over to the other system. And why do we have two systems in the first place?"

"Oh, that's good. Yes, more like that," Rebecca said, enthused.

For the next two hours, Rebecca sat and wrote as ideas flew. Some were terrible, some were too small and finicky to build a business around, but there were some great gems on the list. In particular, a pervasive problem around batch computer processes that a scheduler could solve – she wanted to explore that problem further and see if the issue was as widespread as the squad seemed to think it was.

At the end of the meet-up, Travis pulled her aside. "I don't know if this is a solo project, but if it isn't, I'd be happy to help. I studied entrepreneurship in grad school, and I always wanted to wear that hat."

"I'd like that." Rebecca felt her ears lift with her smile.

The next few weeks were a whirlwind of activity. Rebecca read every book and article on starting up a tech business she could find. She worked through checklists and suggested research steps. She'd send plans and ideas over to Travis for refinement and feedback. She fell in love with one or two plans and then reluctantly had to let them go for various reasons. Finally, she settled on one shining product, with a complete business plan. A plan that included leaving her day job, steady income, and a retirement package, but lacked …

Security, Rebecca mused.

She had been debating it in her head for weeks now. Security offered stability. But it also limited her to the whims of a boss, a company, an upper limit to her income. And yet there was a mortgage, the ever-present Homeowners Association, the country club, car payments, savings (plus match!) for retirement, savings for Tori's college education, and a myriad of other expenses.

If her new company failed, what would they lose, and would it be worth it?

She thought the product was sound. According to her business plan, they would have a product on the market in eighteen months. However, she did these timelines and plans for work all the time, and she knew that sometimes the numbers didn't work, the market crashed, the world got locked down due to a global pandemic, and the future was ultimately unpredictable.

When the numbers didn't work at a large corporation, things like the layoffs happened.

When the numbers didn't work with a small business you started yourself, what then?

She had been driving herself crazy with these thoughts for days. Travis had been getting the brunt of it, and he had been voicing his concerns to her too. They had worked themselves into a spiral of "this is great, it will succeed!" to "this will fail, and we'll lose everything," and it was time to break the cycle.

Rebecca had suggested that they each present the company, the plan, the product, everything to their respective spouses and see what their partners had to say.

So, awkwardly, Rebecca had set an appointment with her own husband for a "business meeting." They set it for one of those rare evenings when they were both in town and Tori was out with friends.

Rebecca wasn't worried at all about what Richard's response was going to be – she knew he would be supportive, but she wanted to get his feedback. His point of view was completely unique from hers. It was one of the reasons they worked so well as a couple.

———

After a dinner at their favorite restaurant, the plates were cleared and the nightcaps were delivered, Rebecca slid the company portfolio out from her satchel and placed it on the table.

Richard automatically reached for it, but Rebecca placed a hand on the cover, gently keeping it in place.

"I appreciate your enthusiasm, but we didn't come here for me to watch you read a report. I want to talk to you about this business, what it is and what it can be. The report is for after, for you to verify for yourself that it is sound. Or not sound, I trust your opinion."

He looked her in the eye and smiled. "It's not often that I see the business Rebecca."

She returned his smile. "Well, here she is, about to make the biggest presentation to the most influential person she knows."

So, she dove in, starting with the problem in the industry.

"Large companies need a lot of computing power every night to run processes for the transactions that occur during the day. We call those 'jobs' or 'tasks.' And if you try to run them during the day, they bog down the whole system and it impacts the whole company, and everyone calls tech support."

"Wait. What kind of jobs or tasks?"

"Like banks. They have millions of transactions like deposits, withdrawals, and point of sale purchases every day that must be processed to the right accounts. Each of those transactions is a job or a task. But it is rare that a bank runs those transactions instantly, the purchase shows 'pending' to your account, sometimes for days."

"And why do they have to run the transactions at night?"

"Because even with technology today, there's a huge amount of data being created, processed, and stored. If you tried to process it all at the same time, your computer network would bog down. Do you remember when you were bored during the pandemic, and you tried to make spaghetti? You put too much dough in, and the machine got jammed? It's like that with data, with a huge bottleneck in processing power."

"I'm never going to live the spaghetti day down, am I?"

"I didn't mention how it tasted."

"True. And that was kind." Richard smiled. "So, every big company has a processing problem."

"Yeah."

Rebecca suddenly realized that common knowledge in her industry was news to Richard.

"But why don't you send the data in real time to India or China where it's night, and their usage is low?"

"Security, mostly. Do you want to hand the Chinese government the banking details of every credit card in America?"

"No. But this is more than just banks, right?"

"Yeah, but security is a universal issue. Privacy and intellectual property must always be protected. Processing power is needed to create special effects in movies and decoding the DNA of the next super virus. These are companies with millions in their security budget. You want to sell a product on Amazon? You submit it to them, and they say, great! It will be available for consumers in 12–72 hours. That's processing power."

"So, if this is such a big problem, what are companies doing now?"

"Paying through the nose for processing power."

"Can't they just buy more computers?"

"Not really. It's not simple – it is manual scheduling; CPU balancing issues and the list goes on and on."

Over the next few minutes, she slowed down and found herself going back and explaining more background detail than she expected. His questions were quite good and forced her to get more granular on the user side rather than the technical side, where she had spent all her development time. She knew that talking with non-technical people was a good thing to do, but she rarely had the opportunity to practice. Now she would have to make speaking 'layperson' part of her repertoire – if she couldn't explain her company clearly and succinctly, no one would buy her products. She wouldn't be able to hire the right people, and if she needed to raise money and couldn't communicate the value, it would make it that much harder.

The deeper her discussion with Richard went, the more convinced she was that there was a BIG problem here for her to solve.

Once he seemed to have a grasp on it, they moved forward to solutions currently in the marketplace, what their strengths are, and what their weaknesses are.

That done, Rebecca dove into the opportunity, that she, with help from Travis, had fleshed out. Her product would harness the power of smaller machines that normally sit idle at night. Her solution would network these computers and add them to an engine that drives the nightly processes. By scheduling the use of these machines to be available when needed, anticipating when the need would occur, schedule backup and redundancies for storms, disasters, and power outages, the solution would be dynamic and solve a lot of the issues that plagued the tech industry. Her product wouldn't just provide the horsepower, but the intelligence to make it wildly efficient and secure.

So far, Richard was still with her, nodding and following along.

She went over the plan, the responsibilities that she and Travis had mapped out, each with their own specialties and strengths overlapping each other's areas of weakness. She talked to him about cashflow, and the contractor work they would be doing in the beginning to make the company have a stream of income on day one. Bootstrapping. There was also a financial projection for the first two years in the folder, but she didn't bring it out.

Instead, she slipped a second, slimmer folder from her satchel and put it on the table on top of the first.

"This is probably more important than the business plan," Rebecca prefaced. "This is our household budget."

Richard looked quizzically at the folder. They each made their own money and had separate bank accounts; they had a fair division of bills to pay from their own accounts. They talked about money regularly but left it to each other to manage the money they each made.

"I pulled most of it from our itemized deductions last year, but if you see something wrong, let me know."

"Did you add in the money I won at poker last year?" Richard asked with a twinkle in his eye.

"Did you declare it?"

"No?"

"Well, I didn't include the money you *lost* at poker either – this budget doesn't include your hobby money."

"Fair enough. I never gamble with household money anyway."

"Just bonuses," they said in unison, smiling at each other for a beat.

"This is a different kind of gambling, you know," Rebecca said softly. "I won't be able to contribute to my retirement, to Tori's education, to vacation savings, any of that for the next year, possibly two. And if things go bad, I could lose everything I invest in it."

"You won't. You work harder than anyone I know."

"I'm going to have to put most of my savings in for startup costs, just to open the doors. Do you know how scary that is?"

"I do. And yet, you're asking a gambler to place a bet on the smartest player he knows." He leaned across the table and gave her a gentle kiss.

"You're out then?" Rebecca whispered sarcastically into his chin scruff.

"Definitely. Too good to be true."

"Beware of a sure thing, and all that?" she teased.

"Come on, let's go home and toast your new business."

The surprise of it all came from Travis. Actually, to be more specific, Travis' wife.

"I'm happy … of course I'm happy to be a dad again," Travis said on the call the next day. "I love being a dad. But I feel like I misled you. I was really looking forward to doing this company, but we can't let go of my health care now."

Rebecca felt guilty. She wasn't happy for him. At least not right away. There was a selfish voice inside of her that was screaming, *You encouraged me and let me think I had a partner, and now you're abandoning me!*

It took a day of panic and a talk with Richard before she was able to see the bright side of all of this. Yes, she was taking on more risk, but she was always the money behind the business in the first place. Travis would have been helpful but paying him from day one would have been an incredible burden for the company. What they really needed were programmers – jobs that would pay for themselves from the beginning.

Now she just needed to get herself clear of corporate life and get her first client.

Luckily, she had a plan for that.

Only the top of Lindsey's perfectly coifed hair was visible when Rebecca knocked on the door jam. She was right on time for her appointment, but Lindsey looked up in surprise.

"Oh. Is it that time already?"

"I'm afraid it is." As Rebecca made her way to the chairs in front of Lindsey's desk, she peaked at the stacks of binders arrayed on the nearly invisible desk. They were all spreadsheets and numbers. Every last one.

The sight of it made Rebecca feel more confident in her decision.

"What is this meeting about?" Lindsey frowned at her screen. "There didn't seem to be an agenda in the calendar."

"Well, it is something of a private nature that I didn't want the rest of the company to see yet. Um …" Rebecca took a deep breath; this was easier in her head. "I've been doing a lot of soul searching, and I've decided that it's time to move on." She paused, waiting for a reaction from Lindsey.

Lindsey just looked shocked. Her eyebrows had climbed an enormous distance towards her hairline.

Rebecca decided to fill the space until Lindsey could get her feet under her. "It's been great working here the last eight years and working for you for the last two. I've learned a lot and I've grown as a leader and a professional. It wasn't an easy decision, but I think I'm ready for a new challenge."

After a brief pause, Lindsey finally seemed to catch up to the reality. "Wow. I'm just really … Wow. I thought you were a company gal for life!"

"I was. And it's only over the last few months that I've been able to see that the passion for my work has moved, and I need to move with it."

"Well, where are you moving to?

"Oh! Great question. I'm putting together a team." Lindsey's face rearranged to object, but Rebecca smiled and quickly reassured her. "Don't worry, all fresh faces, no one from the company. At first, we'll do contract programming and projects for the C-corps. Like that outsource company that is helping on the Fergologic Technologies project. From there, we'll eventually build our own products to solve niche problems in data management. "

This wasn't exactly true. She was deliberately making it sound like her company was going to take a casual stroll down the product-creation road. In fact, Rebecca had a very aggressive timeline to create a new product, and it would be a mad dash to get it launched.

But Lindsey didn't need to know that. What Lindsey needed was reassurance and to come up with the idea that they should keep working together.

"And starting a mom-and-pop shop is really what you want to do?"

The question took Rebecca by surprise. She had expected intrusive "how will you pay your bills", "how with the numbers work" type questions. "Yes," Rebecca answered honestly. "I want to build something for myself."

"Huh," Lindsey sat back in her chair. "Well, since we're putting cards on the table, the fact is, I'm leaving too. I've got an offer to go to Temple-Gordon, and it's too good to pass up."

Temple-Gordon was a major competitor. Rebecca couldn't have been more gobsmacked if Lindsey had stood up and done a back flip. "Really?" Rebecca asked, stalling for time. She had planned on Lindsey offering a contract to her fledgling company. But if Lindsey wasn't here …

"Yes, in fact, I thought you'd end up sitting in this chair." Lindsey gestured towards the stacks of binders on her desk.

Rebecca smiled at the fact that Lindsey thought this job and desk came with binders. She probably thought her next job came with binders too. And Rebecca could tell that Lindsey was testing her, wanting to see if her little nugget of a company could be squashed with a corner office.

And it couldn't.

"I'm flattered," Rebecca said honestly. "If you had asked me two months ago, I would have jumped in while the seat was still warm. But now, I have a new dream I've got to follow."

"Are you sure? This job would have quite the pay bump."

"I really appreciate you thinking of me for it. We've invested a lot in each other over the last few years, and I completely respect and wish I could honor that sweat equity more."

"I get it. But now all my continuity plans here are going sideways. They're going to have to find replacements for you AND me, and I've got to come up with something before I drop the bomb. Do you have a letter? How much notice are you giving?"

Rebecca did have a letter but decided to play her cards out and see where this conversation was going.

"I have it downstairs. It's written except for the effective date. I was planning on two weeks, but I do have some flexibility. Not a lot, but some."

"Could you possibly do six weeks? I need to groom someone to take the reins for both of us, and it would be a lot easier if you were here to help and train. Document some of the processes that are working well with your team."

"I totally get what you need to accomplish. But a month would probably be the most I can stretch this out."

"If you can give me six weeks, I'll make sure contract work at Temple-Gordon gets sent your way. I'll be your first paying client. Plus, it would be good to have a source I can rely on as I learn the teams and projects over there."

Rebecca feigned surprise. "Would you really consider us? That would be amazing."

"Definitely. So … six weeks' notice?"

"Sure! Yes, I'll get the letter for your files today. In the meantime, do you want to brainstorm internal candidates?"

Twenty minutes later, Rebecca was back at her desk, letter completed, and her first client landed. It couldn't have gone better.

Chapter Four

HERE SHE WAS ON HER first day of being a business owner, and she already had a headache. The coffee grinder fired up again, adding to the cacophony of the crowded coffee shop. Rebecca glanced up with irritation. A line of coffee to-go-ers snaked out the door. Rebecca had set up here because Pure Grounds was a city landmark everyone knew. But what she hadn't bargained for was that everyone on the planet would be here at 1 P.M. on a Tuesday, sabotaging all the interviews she was trying to conduct.

The current candidate sitting in front of her was distracted by the noise and the people. His voice had trailed off (again) mid-answer. She leaned forward to hear him, but it was no good. His resume was brilliant, his experience was just what she needed. Personality-wise, she couldn't quite tell. He was introverted, sure. But he didn't really seem to answer her questions. She wanted to like him, wanted him to succeed, but he wasn't opening up.

"I'm sorry, can you say that again?" she asked.

"Success is having code that works – clean, coherent and succinct…" The rest was lost to the noise.

Rebecca decided to push on. "Does it bother you if the user is not happy with what you produce?"

"Well, users are finicky people, and they're not always sure what they want. It's my job to give them what they need…"

Rebecca tried to mentally fill in the blank. She was glad the noise blocked the rest of that response because his attitude was exactly what she didn't need or want. For any company, it wasn't easy to walk the fine line between delivering what the user asked for while at the same time helping them see what they really need. She waited for his lips to stop moving before she thanked him for meeting with her and that she would be in touch …

The candidate looked around, taking in the coffee shop, the grinders, the tables with their crumbs and coffee rings. "I don't think you can afford me."

Rebecca sat back, genuinely taken aback.

"I appreciate you taking the time to interview me, but I think I need to work for a company who truly appreciates talent like mine."

Was it Rebecca's imagination, or did the coffee grinders just stop and everyone heard what he just said?

She felt sorry for his arrogance and was embarrassed by the fact that she had been interviewing him for the last forty-five minutes.

The candidate stood and departed before she could say a word.

And what would it have been? *Sorry I wasted time I didn't have or bought you coffee and pastry with money I need to spend on building my company.*

Her first contract had the ink still drying on it and the money wouldn't start flowing until they hit their first milestone. She hadn't wanted to make the business expenditure of getting offices until she had people to put in those offices. But interviewing in a loud crowded coffee shop didn't bring out the best candidates.

Whoever her first employees turned out to be, they were going to be taking a risk. She needed risktakers to join the team, but they needed to see her vision and be excited at the possibilities, not be looking for a safe bet.

Since the interview had ended early, and the only note about the candidate was NO, Rebecca whipped out her phone and did a quick search. There were a couple of office buildings with co-working space, but that wasn't really what she wanted to build a cohesive team and a secure enough space for a high tech start up. Working alongside other entrepreneurs was intriguing too – good energy and camaraderie. Or would it be too competitive?

No, Rebecca decided. Her target clients were Fortune 500 companies, and she needed to look like a company that they could trust for real, robust, enterprise solutions: not a little startup. At best, her programmers might be distracted. At worst, they'd be prime poaching candidates of other startups in the building.

There were a ton of office buildings within walking distance of this coffee shop, however. She plugged her contact information into a broker's website, just as her next candidate nervously approached.

Rebecca smiled warmly. "Jonathan?" She stood and shook his hand. "Thank you so much for meeting me here." She paused. So far, she had told candidates that the offices were being painted, but it wasn't true, and she didn't want to begin her relationship with any of these candidates based on a lie. "Sorry to meet at the coffee shop, but we're still looking for the right offices. Can I buy you a cup?"

The broker had been a jovial enough guy. However, he tended to ignore budget, pushing her to assume that her business would make enough money to afford whatever kind of space he happened to show. Early in the meeting, he asked her company's name (Branches) and if they had a logo (a stylized decision tree) and then proceeded to point to random walls and say, "Look! Your logo will be on this wall, and you can paint it your brand colors!" Over the course of the afternoon, they went to nicer, larger buildings, which were further and further out of her budget, as he pointed out the walls that would feature their logo.

Rebecca reasserted her budget and her needs and graciously said goodbye at the end of the day. It hadn't been a complete waste, as she now had a firm idea of what she liked (and didn't like) in the area and how much office she could afford. And, she had decided that a huge brag wall that said "BRANCHES" was not in her decorating motif.

Now that she was not going to lie to her candidates, she felt relieved and that she had time to make a sound decision about space.

Choosing her rental space was going to be tough. If she went for cheaper office space outside of town, she might still have trouble recruiting talent. It also wouldn't be good if companies she wanted to work with didn't take her seriously. Plus, space for herself plus two to three employees was needed now. But six months from now? As they grew, she didn't want to constantly be moving and refiling all the paperwork that went along with it.

As soon as she got home, she filled out a pro-con list of what she was thinking for the office. Then she went searching through one listing after another on the web. She was getting exactly nowhere when the front door slammed and the telltale sound of the refrigerator opening came from the kitchen.

Rebecca smiled to herself. It had been years since she was home from the office when Tori came home from school. It was a real treat to see her daughter before dinner.

With a snap of the laptop, she knocked off for the day – or at least until later tonight when everyone else would be watching TV.

Rebecca entered the kitchen as Tori was emerging from the depths of the fridge with her bounty.

"Oh!" Tori apparently hadn't even heard her and of course wasn't used to having Rebecca around either. She almost dropped the hummus from the top of a pile of pre-cut vegetables. "Geez. Give me a heart attack, Mom!"

"Sorry, I guess I should make more noise. Or wear a bell."

"Ha, can you imagine wearing a bell on the stairs?"

"It would certainly get a workout."

"Ding. Ding. Dingdingdingdingdingdingdingdingdingdingding." Tori grinned. "Wait … I think I missed one. Ding."

"You certainly are in a good mood. Did you have a good day at school?"

"Mom. Really?"

"What?"

"You haven't been here to even ask this annoying question in the middle of the day – 'how was your day?' – that's dinner conversation, right?"

"That doesn't mean we can't enjoy trying it while I'm getting the new company on its feet."

"I guess."

"Here, let's try. How was your day, Tori?" Rebecca over-perked her voice, making it sound like she was reading from a 1950s TV script.

"Oh gee, Mom, it was swell." Tori played along. "Mrs. Campbell didn't give us any homework."

"Why not, Tori?"

"Because she forgot to print it out, and she is so old that she can't figure out how to send it via email."

"Wait. Are you serious."

"So serious, Mom."

"That's …sad. How did she teach during the pandemic?"

"She didn't. She took the time off, I think."

"Wow. I feel like you're blowing up my head cannon about Mrs. Campbell."

"I'd tell you to meet her at the back-to-school night, but it's probably past her bedtime."

"Tori!" Rebecca was failing to smother her laughter.

"Yeah." Tori grinned, glancing down at her veggies and hummus. And then she looked back up at Rebecca, seeming unsure.

A heartbeat later, Rebecca realized that Tori actually wasn't looking at her. She was looking longingly at the blank TV screen in the room behind her.

Rebecca felt her heart break just a tiny bit as she smiled and stepped out of the way. Tori had been coming home from school and doing her own routine for years. She didn't need her mom to prep her a snack and was just humoring her by talking about her day.

A few moments later, Rebecca raided the refrigerator and joined Tori in the living room. As a teenager used to being alone, Tori was sprawled out over the entire couch, her belongings exploded out of her bag and now all over the couch and table. Rebecca raised her plate in question. Tori smiled, moved some books, and patted the open space in invitation.

Why oh why did I agree to come here? Rebecca sat in her car looking at herself in the rearview mirror wishing she was back on the sofa with Tori. Part of her mind was willing her to get out of the car and go to this networking event. That part of her mind was rationally explaining that she needed to network in order to understand the local entrepreneurial world and who the players were. She needed to meet peers and maybe find a lawyer, an accountant, and get the inside-scoop on an affordable office space.

The other half of her brain was running in panicked circles. How long had it been since she walked into a room and knew no one – not a single soul? Who would even really be here? People looking for jobs, ones that wouldn't qualify for the kind of specialized work she had to offer. And obviously, the professionals that would be here were here because they weren't the best – those people would be too busy with their thriving businesses. Oh, and people who loved cheap wine and canned cheese. No one would ever know if she left. And she'd be so pissed with herself if she didn't go in there. But if she went in and humiliated herself …

She pulled out her phone and checked the time. She was still a little early. She had time to tame her wild thoughts. Richard was on a flight, but maybe …

I hate networking.

TRAVIS—AIRPORT SQUAD: *No, you don't.*

Then why am I sitting in my car outside of a meeting and not going in?

TRAVIS—AIRPORT SQUAD: *Because your car is more comfortable?*

Haha.

TRAVIS—AIRPORT SQUAD: *Do you know anyone in there?*

Not a soul.

TRAVIS—AIRPORT SQUAD: *That's your problem. Usually, you have a team you already know when you go to these things. Co-workers, competition, sales reps, etc. People you like and hate*

True.

TRAVIS—AIRPORT SQUAD: *Now you gotta go meet these people for the first time.*

> *I don't wanna.*

TRAVIS—AIRPORT SQUAD: *LOL. Somewhere in there is your new me.*

> **Ugh. There is no new you. That's it, I can't go in there. You're irreplaceable.**

TRAVIS—AIRPORT SQUAD: *Absolutely true. But you still have to get your butt in there. Because now you've got your witness. If you don't go in there, you will forever be branded a scaredy pants, and I will tell everyone we know.*

> **Damnit.**

TRAVIS—AIRPORT SQUAD: *Go get 'em tiger.*

Smiling, Rebecca stowed her phone in her purse and stepped out of the car. Travis was right, she was scared because she didn't have a team. And she needed to get over it if she was going to find her team.

A few minutes later, she questioned his wisdom.

After acquiring a nametag, it wasn't immediately clear what she should be doing next. There were quite a few cliques already huddled tight. Perhaps she'd start a conversation while standing in line at the bar? Sure enough, her first chit chat of the night was with a nice gentleman who offered to "buy" her a glass of free wine at the bar. He was friendly enough, but sold flooring, not much to talk about there.

Next, she walked up to a group who were talking about an exciting Multi-Level Marketing opportunity, and Rebecca politely excused herself … nothing against MLMs, but that wasn't her wheelhouse right now.

The next group she sauntered up to turned out to be job seekers, but all she needed right now were programmers, and there were none in that little huddle. She chatted with the group so she could get her voice to work and her feet under her, until the group abruptly broke into smaller conversations, and she was left standing alone. *This is a nightmare!*

"How's it going?" A short bald man with glasses peered up at her.

"Oh, I guess it's going all right."

"What brings you here tonight? I don't think I've seen you before. I'm Stu." He offered a hand and Rebecca shook it.

"You're correct. This is my first time to this kind of thing."

"And what do you do?"

"I own a startup. Programming, data management."

"Wow, congratulations! When did you start?"

"This year, actually." Rebecca didn't want to admit that in fact she hadn't "started" at all yet. That she wouldn't officially start until she had office space and people on the payroll, but gosh it felt like she'd been working at this company for years, just to get to where she was now.

"Do you have any accounting services lined up yet? I have a couple of startups that I work with."

"Wait. Are you an accountant?"

"Yes. Did I forget to mention that?" Stu laughed.

"Well, I was looking for you when I walked in the door then. Do you have a card? And how about a lawyer? Do you know any here that might do well for a start up?"

A tiny klaxon started to blare from Stu's pocket. He looked surprised and then fished a phone out. He distractedly turned it off. "Yes, there are a few great firms in town and one or two lawyers here tonight. Normally, I would be happy to introduce you, but apparently my time is up. My children are languishing in daycare and in need of rescue."

Rebecca smiled and wished him a goodnight. Even if the rest of the event was a bust, he seemed like a nice enough guy.

Rebecca had better luck working the room after that. She began to hear about a female lawyer named Liza that a few people told her she should meet. She looked around the room, trying to read nametags, and she thought she saw a woman that fit the description.

She walked over and elbowed her way into the group. Rebecca waited to be acknowledged and to introduce herself. And … no one acknowledged her. It was the strangest thing. Like being ostracized by the cool clique in high school. Liza even made eye contact with her, and then looked through her and beyond her like she wasn't even there.

Rude.

The group broke up and drifted apart without a single one of them saying hello.

Rebecca wasn't sure if she was angry or … oh yeah, that was definitely anger and massive embarrassment.

"Sadly, you're not the first person to get a cold reception from that group."

Rebecca glanced to her left to where a pint-sized woman with wildly curly hair was smiling sympathetically. "For some reason the lawyers show up to these things, only talk to each other, and slap a restraining order on anyone else who dares to join the conversation." The woman smiled sideways at Rebecca and winked.

Rebecca smiled back. "I'm Rebecca."

"Melanie."

Over the course of an enlightening conversation, Rebecca learned that Melanie was a marketer and social media consultant. She also was a veteran of the local networking scene and very confidently told Rebecca about Fritz, a lawyer who specialized in startup small businesses. She took Rebecca's cellphone number and quickly transferred over the details.

Rebecca wished she could afford a marketing person, especially someone as completely genuine and well connected as Melanie, but until she had a show-ready product her marketing budget only covered her logo. She explained that she needed to be further along in development before diving into marketing, but that Branches would eventually need someone like Melanie once the contracts started coming in.

Melanie smiled and said absolutely, suggesting that they do lunch next week.

"Sure, but instead of lunch, how about a drink?" Rebecca beamed at her.

Melanie replied enthusiastically, "I knew you were my kind of woman."

Rebecca left the mixer feeling hopeful. It felt like the starting seeds of a new tribe, and she promised herself she would grow these new relationships by coming to more networking events.

Chapter Five

"THE COMPANY THAT OCCUPIED THESE offices abandoned the furniture when they closed. So, the building owner apologizes that it isn't empty and 'show ready.'"

Rebecca steeled herself as Jose jingled the keys in the lock.

Jose was a realtor that specialized in office space for startups. He had been introduced to her by, of all people, her daughter. Jose's daughter, Meghan, was on the same tennis team as Tori. Rebecca had been completely surprised and touched when Tori told her about the connection. She was listening and wanted to help!

So far, the hunt today had been going well. Jose had a list of four office spaces to show her, all within her budget and preferred area. He had explained at the beginning of the day that large corporations constantly needed to adjust their space, so often a small group of offices would be on a floor that was dominated by one large business, and of course startups either grew or closed, so there was a quickly changing flow of small office spaces available if you were in the know. He had his finger on the pulse of where those opportunities were for startups needing affordable spaces.

The door lock finally surrendered, and Jose opened the door.

Inside, the office was not the dusty, ramshackle affair Rebecca's mind had populated.

Instead, it was a rather unassuming four-room office with a small nook for coffee. Two of the rooms had a view of the street. One of those had obviously been a bullpen of sorts, large with several desks and chairs abandoned in it. *Perfect for programmers!* The other room with a view was the executive office with one massive desk in it, which she hoped she could trade for two to three small desks. Surprisingly, there was a little executive bathroom there too – just the bare-bones facilities, sink, and mirror. The third room was a receptionist area with chairs that could double as a meeting space. A small coffee nook was tucked in there. The fourth room was a nice small office, room for a desk and a couple of side chairs, perfect for Rebecca's office.

"I like the light."

"I thought you might. That last one was a bit like the inside cabin on a cruise ship."

Rebecca smiled at the comparison. It wasn't too far off the mark. There had been curtains that had opened to a view of the wall. Most of the natural light in that office had come from false walls that stopped a foot short of the ceiling, letting light in from other offices lucky enough to have actual windows. It had been okay now, but she could imagine it being a bleak space in the deep of winter.

This office, on the other hand, had possibilities.

"What's the parking deal here?"

"Permitted in the garage, but the permits are completely reasonable if you can prove you work in the building."

"Do you know if it fills up?

"I'd have to check. There are some guest spots in the garage, two-hour limits. Street parking is also two hours, but there's also a lot on 5th that is affordable."

Rebecca wrinkled her nose. She hated the 5th Street lot. But at least she knew from experience that it would be available if she came in to work late.

Yes, this office is full of furniture, and their corresponding walls scuffed, but it isn't too bad. The furniture actually looks fairly new. "What was this place running again?" Rebecca inquired.

Jose told her.

"Do you think there's any bargaining we can do with that?"

"Yep. Are you willing to pre-pay six months?"

She mentally did the math. "Yes, I think so."

"How soon do you want to take possession?"

"Tomorrow? It would be awesome to do final employee interviews in an office."

"Would you need it painted?"

"By the building people? No. I might want to add some color, but I'll bring in my own help. That's what teenagers are for."

"How about the furniture?"

"I was just thinking about it. Do you think you can work it into the bargain and take the big expensive executive desk and swap for some small desks maybe? I don't have any yet, and these don't look too beat up."

"I bet I can." Jose's eyes twinkled, obviously with the prospect of bargaining for the office space.

Rebecca looked around, took a deep breath, and slowly let it out. "Yep. I think this is it. Let's do it."

Jose left her in the office while he went off to find the building manager. She went into the executive office to use the small bathroom there. As she washed her hands, she glanced down to find a small trash bin brimming with refuse. "I wonder who is going to take out the trash." Rebecca caught sight of herself in the mirror. "Oh, duh." She smiled ruefully at herself. Her company, her trash now. She continued to look in the mirror and wondered if she could juggle all her start up hats. There were many jobs to do and hats to wear, and though she didn't want Richard to know, the janitor hat was one she knew she could handle.

A week later, her team sat in the large office room, working on their first project. It was a huge amount of programming. Travis had come through with a minor job for her team to sink their teeth into, get their feet under them before the real work of Branches began. Lindsey's first project for her budding company was supposed to start in three weeks, plus she was going to need a couple more programmers to work on the new product for the company, not just contract work.

In an ideal world, the team would work sixty percent on contract projects and forty percent on the company product. With more projects, however, there was going to be a need for a bigger team. Otherwise, it would be eighty or ninety percent of her team's time to get the projects done on time, and only minor progress on the real purpose of the company.

With that in mind, Rebecca approached her employees.

Rodney was her lead developer. He had a good grasp of the overall project and experience managing other programmers. He was bald, completely no-nonsense, but if you could get him to smile, he'd light up the room.

Her second developer was Jonathan. Jonathan was the exact opposite of Rodney, tall, skinny, with hair that wouldn't lie flat. He was an extremely efficient programmer and had passed her employment tests with flying colors.

Now she needed to add a few more to the mix, and the candidate she had in mind was ... unconventional.

There was no conference room, so Rebecca had bought the team lunch, and they used an empty desk as their impromptu table. Once everyone had had a few bites, she launched into the crux of the issue at hand.

"So, I have good news. As you know, when I was starting this company, I reached out to several old colleagues to see if they might have some contract work for the company to pay the bills while we develop a solid product to turn around and sell to the larger market.

"The good news is that these guys and gals are coming through BIG time – so now we need to juggle what to take and what to try to delay because our main purpose is building out the Branches product. These contracts are our way of keeping the lights on as we get this company up and going, not the purpose of the company. We are bootstrapping, but that doesn't mean we have to go it alone. We will need more developers ... but I want to go slow and hire them one at a time so we have time to acclimate to the work and see what they can deliver. We can't afford to make bad hires."

Rodney and Jonathan both look a little confused.

"I'm not sure there is room for another person," Rodney said, gesturing to all the empty desks in the room with a smile.

Rebecca nodded, but continued, "Yesterday, I had coffee with a young woman who has literally just arrived from Beijing – her husband is here for graduate school, and she's a software engineer – I was really impressed. She has a standout application and absolutely aced the test I sent out to all the applicants. You guys know the test – it's not easy."

"I feel like there's a catch here," Rodney said.

"It's true, there is. Bao's not great with English and obviously hasn't had any time to practice since she just arrived."

Rodney and Jonathan looked a little unsure.

"She needs a job, and we have a need. She seems to have the skills and came to the interview with a translate app pulled up on her phone and a paperback version of a Chinese-English dictionary. Everything she said and did showed me that she was serious about the job and ready to learn." Rebecca smiled confidently. "To me, she's a talented candidate, but it's not just up to me. I'd like you guys each to interview her; you can use my office. We need someone that you guys can work with as well. And if the team can't work together to help her overcome some of the language difficulties, then we shouldn't hire her."

Jonathan crinkled his nose. "Did you know I visited China when I was in college? I spent a week there. The only thing I remember is how to say is *wô bù dông.*

"Where's the bathroom?" Rodney guessed.

"'I don't know. It's totally fitting that I remember that – because I felt like I said it a billion times to a million people a day. But I also remember how it felt when I got home and suddenly the world was set back to easy mode. It is tough to be that far out of your element. Made me appreciate immigrants a heck of a lot more."

Rebecca nodded, hopeful. She turned to Rodney.

"If she can do the programming, yeah, I can work with her on the team. I worked with a whole bunch of Indian nationals in my last job. It was tough but sorting out a lot of the communications issues in real time without time zone issues will make it a lot easier to trouble shoot."

"Okay, I appreciate you guys willing to try. I do think she's very talented, and worth the extra effort."

"Plus," Jonathan volunteered, "she'll know which Chinese restaurant serves the most authentic food. No more Panda Express take-out for us."

Rebecca winced internally. Was that racist? She wasn't sure, but now she felt like she was going to have to pull out her old company employee handbook to make sure all the anti-discrimination, anti-harassment, and requisite fine print was in place so she could copy it and create one for Branches. Having a diverse company was important to Rebecca so they could continue to attract the most talented candidates. But she was going to have to learn a lot to make it happen.

———

Rebecca nervously checked her video feed again as she waited for the conference call to connect. It would be just her luck that Tori would have left an active filter on the screen and at the start of Rebecca's first official sales call she'd have a UFO over her head or comic booger dangling from her nose. Ah, the perils of the digital world. Her days of flying to sales meetings and Frequent Flyer miles might be gone forever, but there were still sales to be made, and Branches wasn't going to sell itself.

Her little company was growing fast. Their contract work was steady. The guys had interviewed Bao and liked her right off the bat. She had started straight away, and wow was she good. Their fourth employee would be starting in two weeks. That said, Branches was still more of an idea than a product, and her company was more a contract fulfillment firm than an industry changer.

Today would be the first real step in changing that.

She wasn't locked into the Branches product until she had some real interest from the industry. And that meant deposits. Everyone and their mother told you something was a good idea. But it doesn't mean anything if they didn't open their wallet. She wasn't going to spend the next eighteen months building a product without proof of concept.

Rebecca had a slide deck and some mockups from a Fiverr graphic designer for what the interface should look like when it was built. Now it was time to see if it was enough to gain interest and start collecting early orders.

She had set a few calls and sales meetings, but the first to actually come up in her calendar was the corporation down in Florida that Richard couldn't help but point out for their snootiness. They weren't her ideal client, but that was okay because she had worked with them before, and she had a good relationship with them. This would be her first time selling Branches anywhere, and if she blew the sales meeting (which was likely), at least it wouldn't be with her best lead.

The spinning wheel disappeared and was replaced with three heads.

Rebecca smiled warmly at the two men and one woman 600 miles away.

Rebecca instantly felt comfortable. The three on the call were all ones she recognized on sight: Tenisha, Sam, and Ben. It was a bonus that Ben was there; *he makes the decisions that "go somewhere"* – there was always someone like that at every company. They either were hard workers who got things done, or a gatekeeper of sorts, and you had to get their blessing to move on to the next stage.

They exchanged brief pleasantries, and then Tenisha asked, almost eagerly, what it was like to start her own company.

Rebecca had to think quickly, she had prepared to talk about Branches, not her own experience creating it!

"So far, so good," Rebecca said honestly. "It is very different to be out of the corporate world. And at the same time, I'm loving hiring, picking projects, getting things moving. I'm surprised how much progress we've made in only a few months." *Oof,* Rebecca chastised herself. *Don't remind them how new the company is.* "How about things in Florida?" She pivoted. "How is business doing?"

"Well, we already miss working with you," Sam volunteered. "The new you isn't quite ... well, I don't want to tell tales out of school, but let's say we miss you and leave it at that."

Hmmmm, now that's interesting, Rebecca wondered. They had replaced her role with Valarie. *Maybe if they are falling behind, they'll need some contract work.* "Fair enough. But I guess you're interested in seeing what I've been up to." She smiled directly into the camera so each of them would feel like she was smiling directly at them.

"As you know, my company is called Branches, but you're probably wondering why. Branches is a batch computing company that can dynamically direct jobs based on load, volume, and priority." Rebecca shared her screen so they could see her slide deck. "Some of you may have experienced the problem directly or had a programmer come to you and say – on the screen, little speech bubbles appeared – *'It didn't get done because the process hung over night, and no one noticed until late afternoon.'* and *"The job didn't run because a low priority task took precedence.'"* Rebecca knew these were pain points for this particular company.

The others nodded enthusiastically.

So far, so good ... Rebecca continued, "Up until now, schedulers work overnight, when usage is low, so as not to interrupt day-to-day work. However, the current systems out there are not intuitive. They don't understand priority, they can't problem solve and readjust when they run into errors. Each program and system require their own scheduler, and there's no central point that can control all the individual tasks. Each project and program is on its own solo mission, and they often will conflict with each other's goals."

On her screen, an animation of a car trying to maneuver an obstacle course began and quickly drove head-on into the very first barrier. The little driver's eyes were replaced by Xs.

"If they hit a hurdle, they're stuck. And so is every other project behind them."

On the screen, car after car piled up after the first.

"What we need is a more robust batch system. One that can handle large volumes, assign priority, and readjust when they hit a roadblock. One that has a central clearing and prioritization that can streamline the traffic and be more efficient." She paused for effect. "Well, Branches does just that."

The video began to roll again, and this time the little car maneuvered around obstacles called "conflict" and "error." A stream of little cars threaded the roadway behind it. In the car, the little driver smiled.

The next slide popped up with the key sales points.

Branches will:

- Centralize oversight of critical batch processes
- Prioritize essential workflows
- Minimize time spent on routine tasks
- Reduce job failures
- Daily performance analysis and reporting
- Reduce computing overhead
- Certify enterprise security

"I have some mockups of the interface for you, but before I dive into that, do you have questions?" Rebecca asked.

Yes. Yes, they did.

It was a full hour before they got off the call. Tenisha was enthusiastic about the product. Sam asked a lot of technical questions but seemed happy with her answers. Ben was positive, if more reserved. They scheduled a follow-up call with Ben's department head, and with luck it would lead to a beta contract. Rebecca left the meeting wrung out, but happy. It was the best outcome she could reasonably expect.

Chapter Six

RICHARD WAS WAITING WHEN SHE got to the restaurant. Tori was at a tennis meet and would pick up dinner with her friends when they were done. That timing had worked out great, because Rebecca didn't think she could put off the conversation she needed to have with Richard anymore, and it was not good to have a teenager in the mix when talking about money.

"Hey there, sailor. Looking for some company?"

"I'd love to, but when my wife shows up, you'll have to scamper."

"Scamper? Like some poor cartoon bunny?"

"Or duck. She's got pretty good aim."

Rebecca settled into her chair with a wink. "I think I'll take my chances."

Richard had ordered a bottle of their favorite wine and had apparently made a good dent in it while he waited for her. She wasn't that late, was she?

A quick glance at her watch showed her, yes, yes, she was late. Time had been doing that to her lately – skipping forward while she was absorbed in other things. This time, after spending the entire flight back home reviewing Branches' financials, she had decided to detour to the office to review them one more time, then printing them for this meeting.

But now she realized that the time it took to review and print them might have been indirectly proportional to Richard's ability to read them.

For a while, they just made small talk. He told her the news of the day, his meetings, and the latest with Tori.

When it was her turn, she laid out the success of the meeting in Florida and landing her first beta client.

"What! Why didn't you say something earlier?"

"Well, there's some bad news that goes along with it. I was waiting until we both had some food to digest first."

"Ah." Richard looked down at his empty place setting. He quickly scooped a dinner roll out of the basket and ceremoniously placed it on the bread plate, then relocated it directly between the silverware with a small flourish and a makeshift bow. Now it appeared like the lonely dinner roll was his entire meal. "I'm now ready for whatever news you may throw my way."

Rebecca smiled, but felt it freeze on her mouth. *Ugh.* She just didn't want to say it out loud.

"Spill it, Hoffman."

"The company is losing money." She felt a prickle of hot tears in her eyes, but she soldiered on. "I've gone through my initial investment, and we're going to need an additional infusion of cash in the next sixty days, or I'll be out of business."

Richard blinked at her in surprise. "How did that happen?"

"Honestly, the payroll is killing me. I should have hired all contractors, not full-time employees with benefits. And while the contract work is fine and brings in money, it barely pays for the nine to five work and keeping the roof over the company."

Richard pinched off a piece of bread roll, squeezed it between his fingers and deposited the mashed dough on his plate. She averted her gaze as he pinched off a second piece.

"Contract work was never the dream; it was a means to an end. It was supposed to be the bread and butter while we built the real deal. And now I'm having to add contractors to get the contract work done, extra legal fees for the beta contract and graphic work and keeping the team motivated and fed, just other stuff that I didn't budget for, but we need." Rebecca paused to take a breath – it was all now just flowing out of her, and it was a relief to let it all out and be heard.

Richard was all ears.

She continued, "And now we need to get the product into customer hands, solve some real problems, and get some killer testimonials. But when I made my 'infamous' budget, I convinced myself I could do the beta meetings virtually. And that's just not the case. We both know that deals like this are so relationship dependent, and I've not seen these people in months and never as the CEO of my new company. Today's trip was mostly funded by Frequent Flyer miles and no direct flights, but my miles can only be stretched so far, and I need to do four or five more trips to really nail down these beta clients. I'm thrilled that I will have more paying beta clients like today, but those fees are not enough to cover what the actual cost of the product will be. It is a hot mess." Rebecca took a deep breath and let it out slowly. She had come perilously close to a loud, hiccup-inducing, sobbing-in-a-restaurant embarrassment event. She quickly nabbed a bit of Richard's remaining roll and took a generous sip of wine to steady her nerves.

"Well, how much money are we talking about?"

She told him it was high five figures!!!

Richard let out a low whistle. He looked thoughtfully at the ceiling and barely acknowledged the server when their food was delivered.

The silence stretched out as they picked at their food.

"You can't move any employees to contract status?" Richard asked.

"No. I checked, there's laws that prevent it. Plus, it wouldn't be fair to my team – these guys work so hard, have such great attitudes, and are as excited as I am about the future. So no, that is not an option."

"You've got to do the beta meetings in person?"

"Yeah. Today was a perfect test case. I reestablished my relationship and my credibility with these people who are risk averse and need to really trust their vendors – I need to be in the room with them at least once. If I try to do it via video conference, there will be a million more meetings and emails and who knows the outcome. Then I won't have to worry about a budget because I will be out of business."

"Okay, so that one should be pretty easy. I've got my miles too. I've been saving for our next vacation, but it doesn't look like we'll be going on one this year..."

"Oh, I would give anything for a warm beach right now."

Richard smiled sadly at her. "We're too far into this. And I do mean 'we' – it's been so fun and a little scary to see your passion and the unbelievable hours you have put in to get this far. So, no quitting, let's figure this out together."

"Okay, well just so you know, I don't think anyone would hire me now that I have jumped the corporate ship so to speak."

"Really? That's scary, but let's not go there now." Richard mulled it over. "I think the choice is to raid the retirement fund or the house equity. What do you think?"

"I was thinking a second mortgage. But I'm nervous we may not qualify."

Richard scoffed. "We'll qualify."

"We bought the house with two steady incomes. Now I have no provable income."

Richard paused, clearly considering this. "I'll talk to my guy tomorrow."

Rebecca felt a wave of relief pass over her. She might not have all the answers, but she wasn't alone anymore.

Rebecca swore for the umpteenth time that morning. With all the jetting around trying to land beta clients, she had taken her eye off the contract work. And now there was a missed deadline combined with a botched delivery ... for Lindsey.

She was riding her team rather hard to get a functional version of Branches ready so the beta could begin, and the income stream would start trickling in. And now, in retrospect, the issue was obviously predictable. Timelines and quality were slipping for their bread-and-butter contracts.

Rodney rapped a knuckle on the doorjamb.

She gestured to a chair in front of her desk. She turned back to the ALL CAPS riddled email on her screen. In a parallel window was a screen of code. Rebecca forced herself to take a breath and smile at Rodney. It felt a little false, but she genuinely didn't have the ability to make it as warm as she'd like at the moment.

"I'm sorry, I think this is my fault," he said.

"Whoa. Let's not go down that path. We are a team, and we have each other's backs. Clearly something went wrong, but we all own it, and we'll all fix it. Well ... sort of all, because this probably requires coding and I know no one wants me coding." Rebecca could tell Rodney wasn't sure if he was supposed to smile. She tipped him a wink, and he rewarded it with a genuine grin. "I've been doing this type of work for years, so let's figure out what happened and how we can fix it – I will handle the client. Okay?"

Rodney agreed.

"So, give me a rundown of what happened. I've a call set with the client this afternoon. I appreciate your email." She gestured to the screen. "But your frustration was front and center, and so I don't really understand the issues. Also, I love that you shared code with me, but I just need your words to help interpret the issue and what the options are for fixing it."

Rodney explained it to her, and though the details and the way things had played out were a little more convoluted than she expected, the result was about what she suspected.

They had fallen behind on the project. Then in the rush to catch up, assumptions were made, and two independent quality control checks had been skipped, with each person assuming the other had done their check.

So, they blew a deadline, and the delivery wasn't solid. In fact, the program had blown up when the client ran it the first time.

The tension was palpable as she and Rodney walked into the bullpen. Heads popped up, as they all knew what had happened, and it was the first time a delivery had been so monumentally screwed up for a client. Rebecca could instantly see the rest of the team were unsure how she would handle it.

Rebecca pulled up the step stool that she sat on when the team met, as chairs were expensive, and she was bootstrapping everything she possibly could. After all, a step stool had many uses.

"Well, guys, we have good news and not so good news. We had our first beta client install Branches, which is so exciting. It was relatively easy because you put so much work into making a stable product. I appreciate all your hard work on that. However, the not so good news is that it seems we didn't have as much success with our contract client delivery last week. I'm sure there were many things that contributed to this, and I want us to review those, but since I have a call with the client in just two hours, let's start with what it will take to thoroughly fix the issues." She walked over to the whiteboard, her favorite toy, and uncapped an erasable marker.

As they told her all they needed to do, she documented the list on the whiteboard so they could all see it. She then stepped back and reiterated the fixes to them, they added a few more things, and then she asked them to give her an estimate on how many hours each would take.

Rebecca added all the to-dos up, and they all looked at it again.

After a few tweaks, names were added beside the tasks.

Finally, she made a timeline for the entire team to understand and buy into. While this exercise was tedious, in her experience, it worked to keep everyone calm and open. It also kept everyone on the same page, so when she told Lindsey the plan, no back channel between her team and Lindsey's would undermine the tenuous relationship.

They had a few more minutes, so Rebecca then took a small space on the whiteboard to talk about why the issue had happened. It was basically the rush to do more than what was humanly possible to make a deadline rather than push the deadline out a few days or a week.

Rebecca owned her responsibility to the team that she should have asked better questions about how things were going, and she didn't. She also explained that she loved bad news more than bad surprises. "Bad news is finding out the dam is breaking. A bad surprise is waking up to find your house washing away with you in it. Never hesitate to give me the bad news, so I can prepare, repair, and protect us all, okay?"

Most of the heads nodded right away.

She made eye contact with the hold outs, and a small smile, small nod of the head prompted the rest to follow suit. "Oh! And please bring me in when a client calls with a few little things to add to the delivery. We all know 'scope creep' is a real thing, and while that wasn't the reason for this issue, those little addons could cause the next deadline crisis. All additional work, no matter how small, needs to be in writing, particularly with this client. And last," Rebecca reminded them "this remedial work takes priority over all product work."

There was a collective groan, but also a lot of nodding heads again.

Finally, she finished by telling them that client complaints were opportunities to learn, grow and do better next time. And then with a flourish, she pulled out the take-out menu for their favorite restaurant and announced that lunch was on her.

As Jonathan took charge of the ordering, Rebecca grabbed Rodney. They went into her office and closed the door. She had taken photos of the whiteboard, and they reviewed it with a practical eye. Everyone had been eager to correct their mistakes, but the timeline the team had devised was overly optimistic. Rodney and Rebecca came up with what they thought it would really take and then talked about how they could catch the next crisis before it became a crisis. What systems could they put in place now?

A knock on the door to get their lunch order was perfectly timed. Rodney left, and Rebecca had fifteen minutes to breathe and try to anticipate how best to deal with Lindsey.

An hour later, Rebecca wanted to have a good cry and a nap. Or maybe to throw something. It had taken all her self-control to manage the crisis and not feed into Lindsey's histrionics. Rebecca took responsibility – it did squarely land on her and her company. But she was absolutely enraged when Lindsey implied that she only took a chance on her little company because Rebecca had practically begged for the contract.

Rebecca had very politely corrected the record, but Lindsey had said, "Well, I remember it differently." As if that made her dramatic "high school mean girl" routine true.

When Lindsey had finally spent her stream of vile accusations, petty charges, and otherwise vented her spleen, Rebecca explained how her company would be fixing the problem. The resolution really was the only path forward, and she had been apologetic but firm when Lindsey asked for a discount off the invoice. In the end, Lindsey wouldn't settle until Rebecca also guaranteed that she would personally approve the next delivery, which she normally did, but this time she wasn't in the office and Lindsey didn't need to know.

Something has to give.

If she was honest with herself, things were already breaking. She was a good delegator in the corporate world, but she seemed to forget that with her own company. It was past time to relearn how to delegate. She needed the bandwidth to handle issues and ensure quality. But more importantly, leveraging her time was going to be the key factor in growing the company … and finding investors.

Investors. She had looked at her balance sheet from every different angle and there was no getting around it. Her company was bleeding red. She could only invest so much in the company, and they were quickly coming to the end of her resources. If they didn't have investors, they would run out of funds roughly halfway through the beta.

That timeline would be accelerated if she made the hire she was considering.

Rebecca quickly made a list of things that the company depended on her to do on a daily, weekly, or monthly basis. She went through the list and starred any tasks that anyone could do with a little bit of training. She tried to keep everything running and on top of the little details, so the coders could have a distraction-free environment. But check the company spam filter every morning? Anyone could do that! Same with ordering lunch for the programmers and a million other little but essential tasks.

Without hesitation, she wrote an email to her network and told them she was looking to hire a part-time administrative assistant.

Chapter Seven

BRANCHES WAS ONE DAY AWAY from its big debut. Rebecca had decided to introduce the world to Branches by setting up a booth at Enterprise Solutions in Las Vegas. The tradeshow was a huge annual industry event, and Rebecca had decided that she and Laura, her new admin, would man the booth. The team had trained them both on all the product nuances, she knew all the features and those to avoid, and now Laura did too. The team had created some videos to run that could be viewed when she and Laura were busy. Rebecca had reached out to Travis, who graciously volunteered to be the third man on booth duty. She expected things were going to be busy, and she couldn't afford to miss a single opportunity.

Rebecca was doubly grateful that Travis had used his travel miles for flight and hotel. Even with this scant entourage of people manning the booth, this was an expensive outlay for the company. To be taken seriously in this market space, Branches had to be here. Both to attract potential clients and potential investors.

It also (unfortunately) was Tori's birthday, and Rebecca felt terribly guilty to be three time zones away. She had offered to move Tori's birthday celebration to another day, as Rebecca and Richard often moved family holidays since their work travel schedule was so crazy. Tori was used to that, but this time was a step too far, and she made her displeasure clear as Rebecca had left, coldly snubbing her offer of a goodbye hug, and silently going upstairs. Rebecca would have felt better if Tori had slammed the door, but she hadn't. This new Tori was growing up and feeling things on a new, visceral level.

But the show must go on. And what a show it was.

The tradeshow set up was a maze of half-constructed flashy booths with slick people giving directions to blue-collar workers. And it was huge. She made it to the pick-up spot for her booth materials easily enough – that was clearly marked – but as she stood examining the map as she waited for her showcases to be pulled from storage, she knew she would be hopelessly lost. As far as she could tell, they hadn't even bothered to add a "You Are Here" spot to the diagram. However, her map anxiety was quickly proved to be overthinking. Her assigned union of teamsters lugged her cases to her booth space without consulting it once.

They must do this ten times a month.

Rebecca then stood awkwardly as the workers set up her booth and made sure she didn't accidentally create a fire hazard. Occasionally, they would lift something up in a questioning motion, and she'd point to where it should go. While she waited, Rebecca glanced at the other booths that had been constructed so far. She seemed to be the first to get her booth up in her aisle, but that left her with a mostly unobstructed view of the next few aisles over. Most of the set-up booths were logos and brand colors that she recognized, but one a few aisles over was fully constructed and entirely unfamiliar: Octopus. The logo was a bold white font on a field of purple, the color of a new bruise. She wondered what kind of technology company it could be.

When the team was finished setting up her booth, she tried to wander past the Octopus booth, but the hotel workers reined her in. Event policy required vendors to be escorted on the floor until 7 A.M. tomorrow.

She filed a mental note to meander by tomorrow. In the meantime, they needed to get to the bar. Travis had already texted her a picture of a Manhattan, and she absolutely could not wait to catch up with him and introduce him to Laura.

Over drinks, Rebecca briefed Travis on the objectives. First, contacts, contacts, contacts. This tradeshow was her big debut. They needed traffic, demos, and follow-up actions. She had sketched out her follow-up plans on the plane ride to Vegas, and she took Travis through the basics so he could answer questions that might crop up.

Next, she took him though the short list of potential Beta clients that might stop by. It was likely a rep from most of these companies would be here. Even though she had an existing relationship with these Beta clients, their relationship with Branches was still quite new, and she needed to make sure her company put its best foot forward.

"Third," she told Travis seriously, "keep your eyes peeled for deep pockets. If this company is really going to succeed, it needs investors."

Travis assured her that he would. "Are you hard up for cash?" he asked gently.

She needed to be cautious, as Laura was with her, but ... "Yes and no. Cash is coming in, but cash flow isn't consistent yet. I'm struggling to make hires and plan for growth when our monthly income ebbs and flows by 100K. I've started to address it on a couple different levels. I brought on the latest round of beta clients at a higher rate. I renegotiated our terms with some of our contracts for payment due on receipt rather than thirty- or sixty-day pay." Rebecca stretched, trying to project herself as a relaxed, nonchalant boss, "Investors will help raise the overall tide, which will be great. But they'll also open some doors that would otherwise be closed. There are some major C-corps out there that would be great clients, with the right introduction."

Travis nodded. "Wellspring."

"To name one," Rebecca agreed.

"Alright, well-connected investors with money coming out of their ears. Got it. I'll find the guy who will make you a millionaire."

"If you do, I'll put that new baby of yours through college."

"Geez, Rebecca, I would have done it for free. But now that you've promised … no take backs."

She clinked his glass with a smile. "Deal."

———

The next day, the millionaire investor was a far-off pipedream. The location of their booth was a nightmare. She had wondered when the teamsters had set up her booth if it was a bit off the beaten path. But the true disaster hadn't been apparent until her neighbors showed up.

"Who is knocking at your door?" The ominous voice thundered for the umpteenth time that day. A flashy video showed a door caved in. "Malware costs businesses One Billion Dollars Every Year …"

The scare tactic video was obnoxious, but she could sometimes tune it out. Unfortunately, the poor people she was trying to talk to weren't immune from repeat exposure and would break off their conversation to glance at the voice of an angry god booth.

And then inevitably the glance away would be further distracted by the circus that surrounded them on all sides. The booth directly across from Branches had ridiculous cosplay suited people advertising the latest video games. It was attracting a demographic of ten- to twenty-five-year-olds, with plenty of selfies and a constant barrage of "bang bang" video game noise beneath the apocalyptic security warnings.

The booth on their other side was deploying sex appeal to bring interest to their database company. What do low-cut tank tops and high heels have to do with data storage? Nothing, but the women who worked at that booth could literally sweep a man into their orbit with a smile.

Rebecca was simultaneously aghast at the blatant way women were being used as objects and horrified by how effective it was. But combined with the tactics of the others, it was like her booth didn't exist, and that was a definite problem.

Her latest lookie-loo had wandered off. Laura was taking a bio break, and Travis had a tire kicker putting him through the paces on the industry standard and how Branches was different. She stole a quick look at her phone. All her normal day-to-day work was piling up, and she was getting anxiety just looking at it. She had put an out-of-office message on her email, but everyone was assuming she was still going to respond in the normal timeframe. Checking her inbox was like watching a ticking time bomb scroll down to detonation and there was nothing to do about it.

Being 2,500 miles from the office for three days was a risk. The bigger risk was not getting return on the money she had spent on this tradeshow. Rebecca hastily sent out a tweet and an Instagram using the tradeshow hashtag, knowing full-well that it was going to get lost in the noise, and desperate enough to place hope on the internet gods anyway.

Surprisingly, Laura came back to the booth with a prospect in-tow. The more time she spent with Laura, the more confident she was that Laura had been a great hire. She appreciated how she just dove in and started swimming.

Rebecca looked on as Laura exchanged cards, and the prospect took some of the printed collateral. Rebecca knew it was bound for the trash, but not having anything would have left her booth entirely bare and forgotten.

What a waste.

"How is it out there?" she asked Laura when her prospect had departed.

"There's definitely people out there," Laura confirmed. "But the way the tradeshow is set up, people are coming down the main aisle and then filtering through. And they just aren't filtering this way. Two aisles before us, people are going left to this big purple inflatable octopus, or right towards the exit and this delicious-looking buffet restaurant."

Rebecca's stomach growled at the idea of food. She was going to have to grab something soon, and she wasn't going to have time to mess with a buffet.

Her phone goosed her.

RODNEY—MASTER OF CODERS: *SOS Boss. Call when you can.*

Damn it. A bomb had just gone off back at HQ.

Thankfully, Travis' tire kicker disappeared back into the noisy tradeshow floor. She gestured him over.

"I'm grabbing a quick bio break. Can you two come up with a list of what you see working here to attract attention? Stuff that I can feasibly run out and duplicate tonight?"

"Sure."

Rebecca thanked them both and then hurried off to find a quiet place to deal with the latest drama.

It turned out to be an almost comical emergency involving burnt popcorn and a fire alarm. But Rodney had genuinely been convinced that the entire business was going to burn to the ground on his watch. *Poor man.*

But it made her wonder what kind of fire or fireworks would be required to get some attention on the sales floor. Juggling a take-out plate of food when she was walking back into the expo, someone handed the answer directly to her. It was an invitation to an after-hours party hosted by one of the big sponsors.

Rebecca hustled back to the booth with renewed enthusiasm. She waved the invitation at Travis and Laura. "New plan! Go out there, look important, and get yourself invited to as many of these as you can."

———

Rebecca checked her lipstick in the elevator and gave her hair a quick finger-comb. She was on her way to one of the "parties."

She had kicked herself for not thinking early enough of speaking on a panel or in a break-out session, but she had missed the deadline for applying. She had then looked at the sponsorship deck and laughed hysterically. So, like an idiot, she had booked only a booth and not thought much more about it. However, every major player here was hosting private events in the evenings. She could have placed a bet there wasn't a single suite or break-out room not already booked for the length of the tradeshow.

When the hotel elevator doors dinged open, she immediately saw she was right.

The entire floor of the hotel was set up in meeting spaces, and there were any number of people mingling in and out of open rooms with signs showing the companies hosting "parties" non-stop from eight o'clock in the morning to midnight every day of the tradeshow. Some doors had long lines and bouncers checking names, as if it were a club. Others just had perky assistant types with clipboards.

Rebecca smiled politely at a few of these as she pulled out her invitation to one and checked the meeting room name again.

As soon as Rebecca had arrived at the tradeshow, she had seen the opportunity everywhere she looked. Travis naturally looked like a big player who would get the kinds of invites they needed. She had given Laura some of her own business cards, platinum business American Express card and a Frequent Flyer gold card, with instructions to check for her hotel card in her wallet and flash the rest every couple of minutes.

That had left her time to eat, check her emails, and talk to the one person who stopped at the booth to ask questions.

An hour later, the team had come back to the booth with a handful of invitations. And when the tradeshow had wrapped for the evening, they'd made their way to the "high-roller" parties.

Travis was currently working a room somewhere on the 30th floor. Laura was impersonating Rebecca to collect the invites and would be hanging out in some of the hallways, talking up people as they wandered between meeting rooms.

That left Rebecca to mingle with the "party" attendees. She smiled and handed her card to the door attendant. They checked her name against a tablet and then dropped it into a bowl. "For the door prize," the attendant explained.

There was an open bar (she ordered soda water with a lime garnish) and a presentation going on at the back of the room. The event was polished; however, quite obviously, the rush hadn't hit yet. She watched a few minutes of the presentation, introduced herself to the few people not actively watching it, and then excused herself as politely as possible.

She worked the next room much in the same way as the first – card for the door prize, virgin drink at the open bar, working the sparsely populated room. She asked a friendly rep from a small search engine company, which claimed to be a three-year vet of this particular tradeshow, if they were pre-rush or if the rush was somewhere else. The rush was coming, he assured her. But the whole thing wouldn't really kick off until eleven.

Rebecca thanked him but wondered on her way out if by "kick off", the rep had meant party, drinking, and hook ups. She definitely didn't have it in her to socialize until the wee hours of the morning.

As Rebecca made her way to the next event room, she caught sight of Laura in conversation with a woman in a power suit. She was like a duck in water, happily paddling through tide pools of people. All evening, Rebecca had been on the receiving end of a steady text stream of business card pictures with notes about the conversations.

Travis was quiet. Rebecca hoped that was because he was busy making inroads through his invites.

An indeterminate number of rooms later, the crowds had arrived, the music was turned up and the lines at the open bars were long enough that Rebecca didn't have to pretend to get drinks. The live presentations at the back of the rooms had wrapped up and were replaced with flashing screens with core brand information.

Rebecca noticed that she had reached the point where she felt like she had had the same conversation 100 times that night, and that she had no idea who she was talking to. A sales rep? A CEO? It had all blurred together, but she had a satisfyingly large stack of business cards to pore over later, so the "networking" that she usually hated had worked … in a weird way.

Time to call it a night. She left the event, scooping up her phone to see if it was as late as it felt. It was. But right below that was an SOS from Travis sent twenty minutes ago.

TRAVIS—AIRPORT SQUAD: *Octopus party – get over here stat!*

Where?

TRAVIS—AIRPORT SQUAD: *Mezzanine – West Ballroom*

Rebecca hoofed it to Mezzanine level, not knowing what to expect. But if Travis was pinging her, it must be worthwhile.

And it was.

The giant purple octopus inflatable had a fan that waved its arms over a crowded dance floor. A barrage of people stood in line for purple signature cocktails at the open bar. Some revelers had neon purple Mardi Gras style necklaces with octopus arms entwined throughout. Everyone seemed to be tilting from one too many into terrible mistake territory.

Okay, Rebecca thought. *Someone has money to spend on branding. But what makes this party an SOS? Did he meet a VIP?*

She couldn't see Travis, so she ventured a little further in to search. She saw a few familiar faces from earlier in the evening. She smiled and waved as she waded through the crowd.

It only took someone stepping on her toes twice before Rebecca had to admit that she had no idea where Travis was, why she was here, or what she was looking for. She picked a landmark, a presentation screen happening in the far corner of the room with almost no one around it, and texted Travis to meet her there.

And in that corner, Rebecca felt the floor drop completely out from under her. In dumb show pantomime, the screen showed a cartoon of an octopus at the central hub of a network with each arm distributing jobs to computers in its reach.

It was a visual, violently purple, and extremely memorable depiction of her own Branches product.

Chapter Eight

"I THOUGHT YOU RESEARCHED THIS?" Richard asked over the phone.

"I did!" Rebecca said. "They only just popped up as a company in the last quarter."

Travis had found her in the hallway outside of the party, trying to hold her internal pieces together. He had filled her in on what he learned. Rebecca wished he hadn't been so calm and straightforward as he gave her the details. It reminded her of the practiced solemnity of a doctor giving a terminal diagnosis.

"So, what does this mean? Did someone beat us to the punch?"

Rebecca had been turning that over in her head too. "I'm not sure," she admitted. "The company certainly has better funding than ours, deeper pockets for resources. But I don't know how close they are to having a viable product. We might actually be ahead of them in development."

"Is there any way they could have stolen your idea or your IP?

"No. Definitely, not. And it isn't totally crazy that there would be two break-out companies going after the same market at once. There is a huge need to update outdated tasking software. The original programmers of BMI are retiring, and PROCESS was written in a programming language no one speaks anymore. Someone else was bound to see the opportunity."

"So ... then what's next?"

Rebecca looked around her hotel room, wishing she was home. She had called Richard without looking at her watch "I don't think anything has changed. I need to step my competition research back up, so there's that. But I don't think the strategy changes. And in the short term, two more days of tradeshow. Ugh, just saying it makes me tired to my bones."

"I'm sorry. Is there anything I can do to help?"

"Other than answering a 3 A.M. call when your wife is coming apart at the seams?"

"Yes, other than that."

"Just give Tori a hug for me tomorrow. I miss you both."

"I know you've got a lot packed into your days, but if you could call around five, you should be able to wish her a happy birthday before the rest of the teenagers descend."

"I will," Rebecca promised before hanging up. Her hotel room felt very, very lonely.

Rebecca was nurturing a cold, exhausted, and unsure what to expect when she got home on Sunday. She had managed to call Tori (after seven) and got a cold reception. Apparently, she was interrupting some unspecified but very important birthday activity, and if she wanted to know details she should have been there instead of Las Vegas. It didn't matter that Rebecca was there for foot-sore, indentured work that might eventually pay for Tori's college education.

Rebecca wondered if she was turning into Lindsey. She had been locked in her office with spreadsheet after spreadsheet. Her eyes felt grainy, and more than once she found her nose absurdly close to the paper. How can it be this bad?

After her trip to Las Vegas, things were supposed to be better. But the leads the event had managed to generate had not materialized into customers yet, and the soft launch would go live next week with hardly more clients than the beta.

Her books were looking anemic, bordering on red, red, red.

A gentle knock tapped at her door. Rebecca looked up startled. *Is it 2 P.M. already?*

"Am I interrupting?" When Don smiled, the tan lines from his sunglasses crinkled.

It made Rebecca a little jealous that he had time to get sun at all. "No, no. I was actually prepping for this meeting and got lost in it."

Don was her fractional CFO. Stu, the accountant at the networking group, had introduced her to Don, and it had been a good fit. Don had cut his teeth working his way up in the corporate world, then went independent to help companies like hers make the transition from start-up to establishment. He had successfully helped two companies raise money and helped a third one through a sale to an acquiring conglomerate. A few years from now, he would be out of her price range, but right now he was building his portfolio. She was lucky to have him.

"I was working on the pitch deck and got sucked into the numbers." Rebecca gestured for him to sit at the table adjacent to her desk. She hated meeting people at her desk, as it felt too "called to the principal's office," and no one could relax. She grabbed her spreadsheets and notebook and joined him at the table.

Rebecca immediately handed him the in-progress pitch deck. She had all the basics that the million webinars, podcasts, blogs and "how-to guides" said she needed to have. The company overview, competition, and target market were all business 101 requirements. She could have written those slides in her sleep. She had invited Melanie, the marketing consultant she had met at the networking group, over on a slow afternoon to take pictures of the team for the "team" section, and Melanie had also helped come up with a more professional looking design for the overall deck.

The parts of the deck that frustrated Rebecca were the future pieces. She had projected her departmental budget, milestones, and finances a million times for others. But for her own company? The stakes were high, she was second guessing everything, and there was no corporate safety net that she had never before appreciated. Was she being too ambitious? Not enough? What would a potential investor want? What would they be skeptical of?

Rebecca had gotten a little too far down the rabbit hole and created three different sets of projections for Don to review and offer his professional opinion. She had expected that he'd go for the middle one, but he surprised her by going for the most aggressive version.

"That first one isn't a big stretch, and you want to show the investors a good return on their money. If you aren't trying for a big return, they definitely won't get it. The second one is more of what they are looking for. But the highest one is still practical, achievable without being too pie-in-the-sky. I think your corporate years trained you to be realistic. And most entrepreneurs are too optimistic, and the projections are wildly overblown. So even though this aggressive projection is going to be tough to achieve, compared to the other companies like yours, this one seems grounded in reality."

After a little more back and forth, Rebecca made a few tweaks to the final projections and entered them into the pitch deck. She was excited because it felt like one of the last pieces of a puzzle sliding home. She had really wanted Don to do the projections, but she knew she needed to know the numbers inside and out in order to answer questions and the only way to do that was to build them herself.

Don cleared his throat. "If you don't mind, I've been dying to give you the good news since we started."

"Oh! There's good news? I'll take it!"

"My lawyer friend called with another prospect, so we have another possible investor on the line."

"Cool! What do you know about him or her?"

"Not much yet. Just that her name is Louise and that she recently sold her education company. She is apparently keen to invest in other women-led companies."

"Well, I like what I'm hearing already." And privately, it absolutely boggled her mind that loose networks of people were contributing to the success of her company. She had used similar networks in her previous career, but to see how it was coming together for Branches was just … amazing.

"Yeah, I think it will be a good fit."

Rebecca flipped to the potential investor list in her notebook and added Louise and the scant details they had so far. "So that makes …" She quickly did the tally. "Nine potentials. I'd really like to get a few more meetings set up, just in case a few decide not to invest."

"Speaking from experience, you have ten meetings and three will ask for more information about something we can't predict because they're all different. Three will be excited and ask for the term sheet and legal docs, three will ask about the minimums and the maximum they can invest, and one will just say this is too early for me or it doesn't fit my portfolio at the moment or something that is actually just a NO. It's a bit of a roller coaster, but you're a master at roller coasters, so you'll answer their questions, promptly and thoroughly, and I'm here to help if needed. Then the really serious people will have someone on their team review the latest books and cut a check." Don wrote an invisible check with a flick of the wrist.

Rebecca's mind was boggling, but in a good way.

Don continued, "Then there'll be a percentage that hem and haw, and they'll tell you they need to think about it. You keep following up, and eventually they'll buy in at 10 P.M. on a Tuesday. I don't know why it is 10 P.M. on a Tuesday, but it inevitably works out that way." He performed a shrug. "As long as the money clears, it works out."

Rebecca wholeheartedly agreed.

"But then, some that asked for more information might want more meetings, more documentation, new projections, and they will kick the tires, kick the tires, kick the tires, and never get on board. There is only one tactic I know to move these people to make a decision, and that's to set a deadline once you've got your first check in hand."

She felt her eyebrows try to touch her hairline. "A deadline? Like give us your money by 5 P.M. Friday or we won't take your money?"

"Sort of, but you say we are closing the round on x date – deadlines help drive decisions."

"But I want their money. What if they come to me on Saturday and want to give me money?"

"It might happen, and of course, you can take their check or wire, but you need to be firm, as some are never going to invest, and you have to stop chasing them. Remember, they have all the time in the world, and you don't. Your clock is ticking."

"So, I do my presentation meetings and then say, 'drop the cash in a bag at the reception desk by 5 P.M. Friday or else,' and that works?"

"Yeah. Usually, the deadline is the end of the month. Or the 15th. You say you're closing the round, and if they decide not to participate in this round, you thank them and put them on your 'maybe list' for the next round. You need to show you're serious, that you have a business to run, and you know what you're doing. Many investors like to come at the last minute, and at 4 P.M., you'll think it was a failure, and by 5 P.M., it'll be a success."

She rubbed her temple. "You must have nerves of steel."

"Maybe. But you hired me, so trust me. This will make the players buy in, and the tire-kickers will go home. It will save you so much time in the long run, I promise."

Rebecca felt a nervous tension in her gut. "Okay, but do we want these people as investors? We are certainly in need of money, but we also need those who can help us and align with our values and who will not be micromanaging me and the company to its demise?"

Don looked at her and asked, "How do you know that this is so important? Most of my clients balk when I tell them that they need to do the same due diligence on their investors as the investors do on their company, and its usually an uncomfortable battle."

Rebecca laughed. "Actually, you told me in an indirect way when we first talked, but I got the message. It made sense to me in a weird way, and now I'm so glad you did tell me, as I don't want to fall in love with some crazies with deep pockets."

"Well, I feel gratified that you listened to me on that. And you should also listen to me on this. You said your husband likes to gamble, right? This is your turn at the table, and you've got to hold steady until the end."

Rebecca smiled. "I think I can do that."

———

Rebecca was startled by a soft knock on her door. She'd been in the zone, trying to figure out where her next sale was going to come from. The soft launch of Branches' product had given the company four sales so far this week. She had lined these clients up months ago and was pleased that the work was paying off. But four companies weren't going to pay the bills. She needed to find more prospects, set up more sales calls and shorten her sales funnel.

A big corporation took months to pull the trigger on new software. She had to refill the pipeline if Branches was going to have a healthy bottom line.

"Come in," Rebecca called at the door. She made a hasty note, so she wouldn't lose her place.

Laura peeked her head in. "Do you have a minute?"

"Phone call?" Rebecca asked. "Someone wanting to invest millions?" She hastily dropped Laura a wink to let her know she was joking. For a moment there, Laura had looked absolutely horrified that she had interrupted at all.

"Well … the rollout, as you know, has had some rough bits. I've seen the team really hammering down to fix the installation bugs and smooth out the customer transition of tasks. It looks like they finally nailed down the import feature that was having the compatibility problems."

"Really?" Rebecca glanced at her computer to see if she had missed an alert.

"Yeah. I think they cracked it last night."

While Rebecca had landed four clients this week, the rollout had not been smooth. From purchase to installation, to initial use, Branches had been plagued by issues. Particularly when a company had a robust set of processes that needed to transfer from the old system to the new one. Each corporation had their own hardware, outdated software, and a myriad of difficulties that came with each scenario.

It was difficult to pre-emptively figure the issues out, so Branches wasn't a "plug and play" yet. And when corporations were paying near-full price, they had expectations that things would run smoothly. A smooth onboarding would create confidence, and so far, her performance in this area had been lackluster.

"I wonder why they didn't tell me."

"You know them. Probably just moved on to the next problem."

Rebecca smiled. "Look at you, this is all old hat for you now."

"I definitely have a feel for the ropes, which is why I need you now." Laura tilted her head to indicate the larger office outside.

Rebecca felt her eyebrow tilt in confusion. But what the heck, she was game.

Jonathan, Bao, and the rest of the programming team were standing awkwardly around an unused desk. On the desk sat a stack of Dixie cups, probably nicked from a bathroom, and an unopened bottle of champagne.

Rebecca glanced at Laura quizzically.

Laura smiled and efficiently started uncorking the bottle of bubbly. "Branches hit a milestone earlier today. And I think everyone here was so busy doing the programming and the work it takes to make this company go, that no one realized that it happened."

Rebecca was bemused to see several confused and furtive glances around the room. They matched her own.

Laura beamed at them all. "This morning, a client signed up. They got their welcome email. Their instructions. They followed it immediately, which we all know is a miracle in and of itself. They downloaded the software, and their system was remarkably similar to one of our beta clients, so the installation went off without a hitch. They used the new import interface, which was just completed last night. And the interface ... worked perfectly. The verification tasks came back green across the board."

The champagne cork came free with a satisfying pop.

"My friends and colleagues, we have a working, viable onboarding and installation process!"

There were a few cheers and claps around the office. It didn't feel like nearly enough.

Rebecca took her cue. "It has been a lot of hard work to get here. And before I really toast to that, I want to first thank Laura for taking the initiative to make us stop and appreciate the moment. Not everyone would see these milestones, and very few would run out and buy a bottle of champagne. So, I want to first raise a Dixie cup to Laura for taking the initiative. We need to stop and appreciate the moments more often."

There was a "here, here" around the office.

"Okay. Now I need to thank all of you. You've been pulling double duty fulfilling contracts and building Branches at the same time. You've been logging the sweat equity with Branches, and I want you to know that I see you. You've endured long hours and some truly terrible take-out. By the way, did someone finally shred the menu to Gino's?"

Someone shouted an affirmative and there was a chuckle around the room.

"Good, that place was awful. And you? You all have rewarded that bad take-out with dedication and persistence that has gotten us to this day.

"So, I want to acknowledge it isn't easy to join a startup. It takes a certain kind of person who signs on for a vision and goes on to have faith that the paycheck will follow. Who eats the bad take-out and buckles down to get the work done. I appreciate that faith so much."

There were smiles and nods as her staff sipped from their Dixie cups.

"I'm very proud of where our little company is today. It took a whole team to get us here, and I want you to know that I see you, and I see your contributions. What you've added is amazing, and your enthusiasm is immeasurable." Rebecca held her Dixie cup high. "So, thank you."

"Thank you," came back to her from many voices, many contributors.

Rebecca felt herself tear up slightly. This was her team, her supporters, her 'tribe', and she couldn't have felt prouder of them all. She sipped her champagne and smiled as the rest of the team did the same. They really were exceptional.

Chapter Nine

REBECCA SAT NERVOUSLY IN FRONT of Louise, her potential investor.
The presentation had gone as planned, exactly like the previous meeting.
But the first meeting had been with an acquaintance, and Rebecca felt,
perhaps naively, that it was a virtually guaranteed investment. It had been
hers to lose and she had delivered the presentation flawlessly and got the
check in the room.

Louise, however, was a different story. The relationship was barely warm,
and the only thing in common was interest in the investment. It was hard
to build rapport when you knew it was in service of getting a big check at
the end. Still, Rebecca was doing the best she could to build something
genuine here.

And Louise was intimidating, whether she intended to be or not. Rebecca
guessed that she was maybe only a year or two older than herself. But Louise

had already built a learning software business named HereThereLearn. It had state-of-the-art learning technology AND security, and she sold it for millions.

Rebecca had delivered the presentation, and now she found herself fielding questions like an amateur. They had gone through her current financials a second time. She felt embarrassed about those because she had worked so hard to be agile and frugal, yet the books were barely scraping black.

"And these projections, what assumptions did you use for them?"

"Assumptions? Like … the number of clients?"

"Yes, I think we should dig in a bit deeper on all of them. I know when I was building HereThereLearn that the assumptions were what would make or break the success of the company. Too aggressive, and I wouldn't make the target and would result in an unhappy board of investors. Too conservative, and I'd be leaving money on the table. I'd like to see where you're falling in the spectrum and how you got there."

Rebecca mentally scrambled. "My assumptions are a bit on the conservative side, but I don't have the details ready to show you today. I'll prepare a report and send it to you before the end of the day?" Her voice rose at the end, turning her confident statement into a question.

"Tomorrow would be fine. However, I'm surprised that you couldn't give me the assumptions off the top of your head. You told me you built the model. So, are you just exhausted and nervous … and it's getting in your way?"

Rebecca forced herself to breathe past the lump in her chest. She didn't trust her voice at the moment, and so she just nodded. Better to be thought nervous than incompetent.

Louise continued, "I am happy to wait to see them, but you really need to figure out how to compartmentalize your thinking before you sit with a potential investor or customer, so you can clear your mind of all the problems and crises you deal with when running Branches day to day. There are lots of tricks for doing that. I use a virtual box, and I imagine all the day-to-day issues streaming into the box, which I then put a lid on. The problems are still there to deal with later, but they are out of the way so I can focus on the task in front me. Try it, or something similar, and see what works for you."

Rebecca felt a stab of disappointment that she wouldn't be closing and getting another "in room" check again. But she knew better than to let the disappointment show on her face.

"Are there any other questions I can answer for you now?"

Louise asked her to go over a few more points from earlier in the presentation. Rebecca wondered if she had let her nerves get the better of her and gone too fast in her delivery. Louise then asked if she could have a copy of the presentation as well. So maybe she was just very thorough and cautious?

"Okay, so I'll send you a copy of the assumptions and the presentation to you by the end of day tomorrow. And thank you again for bringing up the details for the assumptions, I would love a set of experienced eyes to give me feedback.

Louise smiled mildly. "If the reports look good, I'm in, so please also send me the closing details."

Rebecca felt her heart take an unexpected lurch. She tried to return a normal smile, not a manic grin. "Thank you."

"For what it's worth, I've been in your shoes. I think you're doing great."

Rebecca let out a breath she didn't know she'd been holding. She felt herself tearing up. It was a tiny bit of empathy she hadn't even known she needed. "Thank you."

————

As it turned out, nearly every other investor meeting had asked for the logic behind the projections. They all wanted to know how the sausage had been made, and because Louise had graciously nudged her down this path, Rebecca had used the trick of an imaginary box for her problems, and she had been more than ready. More than one prospective investor was happy she was so well prepared.

Rebecca was mid-pitch in her penultimate presentation for this first initial round of fund raising. She had the report on the table, ready to slide it over when the prospect questioned her projection methodology, but something had been off since the beginning of this meeting.

The investor was the nervous one this time. Albert was a friend of a friend of her accountant, Stu. He had apparently made a tidy bundle in electric car charging stations. At the beginning of the meeting, he had spilled his coffee almost immediately and then apologized so profusely that it had bordered on awkward comedy.

She checked herself and wondered if she was becoming over comfortable asking people for money. But she wasn't swaggering, throwing money around, or being blasé about the investment or the company. No, she wasn't putting off any strange warning signals. Albert was just a mess of nerves.

Rebecca reached the point in the presentation where the prospect typically asked for the underlying assumptions behind the timeline. She paused.

Albert cleared his throat. "Uh. I can tell that you have a very good, well-polished presentation."

"Thank you."

"How did you get interested in all of this?"

"Entrepreneurship?"

"No, programming. Lots of women start companies, make-up, and such. It's rare to see a woman running a software company."

"Oh, probably the same way a lot of men get into it." Rebecca flashed Albert a smile. "Businesses have problems, and programming is a very specific tool set for fixing them. You understand the tools in the toolbox, and you can build anything, fix anything. Then it is just a matter of picking what problem you want to solve first."

"Ah, I like that. A toolbox, very clever. I got into car charging because I could see the coming need in the marketplace. Someone was going to make a fortune on charging batteries, why not me? But here's my question to you. Do you think there's a fortune to be made in batched job scheduling? It's not something the public is banging down the door to buy."

Rebecca took a beat to collect her thoughts. "You're right, the public isn't banging down any doors for this. But I'll tell you who is, corporations. Because they have one, sometimes two programmers left in the whole company who are trained on their existing batched software. It's written in a complicated, dead programming language, and all the soon-to-graduate computer science majors are making phone apps. No one imagines a career in data management. And in about six months, those last few programmers are headed out for retirement. Corporations need a plug and play solution, one that has a point and click interface, and they need it yesterday."

Albert considered her, and Rebecca wondered how she could have thought he was nervous before. He wasn't nervous, he was testing her. And she didn't like it, at all.

"Before I make a decision, would it be possible to meet the board of directors?"

"The board?"

"Yes, I want to see who I'm getting into bed with, so to speak."

"Oh. Well, there isn't currently a board of directors. There will be after the funding round is completed, but there hasn't been a need for one up until now."

"No board at all?"

"No, but there will be shortly. May I ask, have you previously had a bad experience with a board of directors?"

"Oh, no. No. I just find that they hold the actual power with a company, and so I want to make sure there's someone looking out for the money there. You never know when someone will have a bright idea to overspend the investment. But if you don't have a board …"

"The investment will be spent according to the budget laid out in—"

Albert waved her off. "And one day the payroll is short, and you have to pull money from somewhere. I know how it goes."

Rebecca flushed. Had Stu said something to Albert? It had only been one time that she'd had to rob Peter to pay Paul. And all of that happened before she'd ever hired Stu to mind her books. *There's no way either one of them could know about that, could they?*

Albert grinned at her, knowingly. "Money gets tight, you need tight controls to get you through. I want a board to hold you accountable. And if there isn't one, I don't think we're a fit."

Rebecca felt a tight smile on her face. "I understand. If you'd like, I can put you on the list for the next round of funding."

———

"He made me feel this tall!" Rebecca showed Richard her fingers, a centimeter apart.

He winced in sympathy.

"It was beyond humiliating. He was a dyed-in-the-wool misogynist, and I was having to ask him for money." She took a swig of her wine. "I don't have enough words for how insane that whole meeting was. I had to take a shower when I got home."

Richard had been smart enough to see that when he got home, and rather than ask what's for dinner, hastily suggested they go to dinner. Tori was at a friend's house, and so it was just the two of them.

Despite the restaurant and the lovely company, Rebecca still couldn't let it go. It was like this brewing anger in her body.

"It just boils me – he was right, you know. I did nick the money from the payroll tax account to make the payroll. Just once, back when we were trying to get the second mortgage on the house and the closing was delayed. And as soon as the money was funded, I replaced the balance."

"You did what?" Richard seemed genuinely shocked. "Why didn't you tell me this before?"

"Deniability. If I was going to go to jail for tax fraud, I wasn't going to have you go down with me. Someone has to raise Tori."

"But the money was replaced," Richard asked. "No harm, no foul, no one is going to come knocking on our door?"

"Right. I replaced the money and the taxes got paid in full on schedule."

Richard held a hand to his heart. "Jeez, you almost killed me."

"What I don't understand is: how he guessed? Does every entrepreneur do this?"

"Maybe they do. But, Rebecca, don't do that again. We can find the way with our own money next time. This company isn't important enough to go to jail over."

"I absolutely wish we could self-fund this whole thing. I hate asking for money."

"Can we?"

"No. We're going to have to tighten the belt as it is. We thought by now I would be bringing in close to my previous income. And I can barely cut myself a paycheck on a regular basis. I don't think my paycheck even covers the monthly country club dues. What would you think about taking a leave of absence or whatever they call it when you can't afford it in the short term."

"Ooof. Any chance we can hold off making that change until after the poker tournament next month? Maybe I can win enough to pre-pay the rest of the year."

Rebecca did the math in her head. Part of her wanted to shake Richard. They could quit the country club, and he could get Tori tennis lessons for a fraction of the membership cost. But they had agreed that his bonus money was his money to gamble, if he decided that's what he wanted to do with it. She couldn't go back on that now because her company wasn't raking in the money yet.

"I guess," she said. "Do I want to know what the buy-in is?"

"Nope, but I already paid it, so it isn't an extra expense. We just still need to be members in good standing when the tournament happens. You know, that actually gives me an idea that might help. You should get an investor to double down."

"Double down?"

"Yeah, like get them to invest double the money. Since the investor today is a 'no,' it can make up the difference."

"Like double your money, double the payout?"

"Yes. These people have the money, you just have to give them an opportunity to double down on you."

The problems of the day didn't feel so big anymore as Rebecca's mind whirled with the possibility. Could she convince someone to do a double investment? Well, she had one more chance to try. Her last appointment for this round was tomorrow afternoon.

"I don't mean to talk too much about myself, my achievements are pretty unbelievable. But I do have software experience and have sat on the board of some noteworthy companies," Arun said.

Rebecca schooled her face into polite interest. Since she started counting, this was the fourth time this potential investor had self-aggrandized. And yes, her due diligence had uncovered Arun's extensive career – he had a lot to be proud of – but his need for self-promotion kept derailing the presentation. At the beginning, she had engaged him and patted his ego. And it hadn't been enough. An hour of allotted time was gone, and at this point she was usually into the open Q&As. She still had half her talking points to go.

Rebecca would have cut this off thirty minutes ago if this hadn't been her last potential investor. Improvising, she picked at the latest thing Arun had said and redirected the conversation. "Branches will be forming a board within the next month. If you're interested in sitting on it, there will be an additional reference step for due diligence. After all, we need a board that will be able to work together to steer the company in the same direction."

"Oh, yes, yes. I have plenty of references. Even a few smart ladies like yourself. I have helped advise some great companies achieve remarkable success."

Fifth time. She wondered if Arun was a flat-out narcissist or if there was a particular response, he was looking for that she, one of the ladies, hadn't given him. Or maybe he was just like a particular blue cartoon fish that couldn't remember the conversation halfway through. She redirected to her presentation this time. "Our success right now is a humble start. We have a working product, an initial base of customers, and a plan to grow." Rebecca took him through the details and made herself practice all her patience. As he would derail, she would pick up on the last word he said and work it into what she was saying next. It was tedious, but it made her pay attention rather than tune out.

If Arun was as successful as he bragged, he would be a good contribution to her company. He would understand the problems that she was trying to solve, and he would be desperate to continue adding to his own success. A year from now he'd be bragging about how he succeeded with her company to some other captive audience. That was tempting.

The ultimate flex came when they reviewed the initial investment figures. Rebecca had been prepared to "double down," as Richard put it and sell a seat on the board, if need be, to get the extra cash. Arun, however, beat her to it.

"This initial investment figure that you have listed, this doesn't work."

"Oh?"

"No, it is about half the minimum that I invest when I come to a new business. Small investments aren't worth my time, and playing small ball only gets you small results. If I make the investment, I'll need to invest more." And he named a number roughly twice her asking price.

Rebecca smiled. "And in return for your extra investment, you'd be looking for a seat on the board?"

"Yes, a guaranteed seat."

Rebecca nodded, considering. "Before I accept that sort of deal, I really will need a list of boards you've been on and speak to the entrepreneurs involved. I'm fine with accountability and growth opportunities that come with a board, and in fact, I am very excited to begin. But how personalities work together matters to me, and I want this to be a 'can't wait to meet with the team' environment."

Arun assured her that his contributions lead to success. If she believed everything he implied, then it sounded like Arun was going to single-handedly code her product and market her business. In her experience, that kind of bragging was a warning flag that he would do nothing but sit back and watch the returns come in. But realistically, what did she expect? What did she need?

Rebecca needed money. She needed a board that had experience and could open doors to opportunities she wouldn't necessarily have.

She smiled. "One of the other duties of the board members will be to make introductions and help Branches break into industries we don't currently have a market share in. High transaction batching industries, like banking."

"Oh yes, I have a great many friends we can speak to about Branches. Have you considered Microsoft."

Okay, Rebecca thought. *This might work.*

Chapter Ten

THE LIGHT RAP ON HER door was followed by Laura's head tentatively peeking in. "I'm sorry to interrupt …"

Rebecca hit 'save' on what she was doing and waved Laura in further. She had been neck-deep in problem-solving, but Laura interrupted so seldom that it was likely worth it. "What's up?"

"Do you remember you telling me that when the first board of director meeting is scheduled that you were going to need a lot of time to prep it … and you tend to wing things … and that you can't wing this one?"

"Yes."

"And that the investor reports are going to have to be perfect and you couldn't throw them together in a rush – this had to be a polished document to build their trust in you?"

"Yes." Rebecca felt a twinge of uneasiness.

"Well, through a fluke of scheduling, the meeting and the reports are due on the same day."

"Please don't say it is tomorrow."

"No! Nothing that bad. I wouldn't do that to you. But the big day is two weeks from today. And I have no idea what you need, so I'm here to let you know you need to tell me what to do."

"Two weeks. Okay, we can do this." Rebecca thought for a moment. "This is good because I have more questions than answers right now. Do you have a minute? Let's map this out."

Rebecca had installed a wall-to-wall whiteboard in her office as soon as she had settled in. She took a quick picture of the notes currently up and then did a quick spritz and wiped it down. Rebecca smiled at a memory of a conference a long time ago that had been conducted entirely on the whiteboard. The presenter did her talk, and behind her, a very talented cartoonist live drew the key components of the talk acted out by various characters. The presentation and the content were impressive, and then Rebecca had been lucky enough to be seated by the presenter at dinner that night. She and Liz had become good friends after that.

Liz checked in with Rebecca from time to see what she was up to. Rebecca suddenly realized she hadn't updated Liz on leaving the corporate world. She kicked herself mentally. How could she forget Liz? She would have been so excited to hear about everything Rebecca was up to – and she sat on enough boards that she probably counted board packets instead of sheep at night.

With a quick uncapping of the dry marker, "Call/Email Liz – Advise on Board Packets" topped the list. It was quickly followed by "Agenda for Board Meeting" and "Where to hold board meeting."

"Laura, can you text Don and see if he's available to pop by? I think we're going to need a lot more experience in the room just to know what we don't know."

An hour later, Don was in the room and adding his experience to how best run the first Branches' board meeting. He even brought a board packet from a previous client, and the meeting outline was ...*huge*.

Rebecca reached for it, only to have it protectively removed from reach.

"Sorry, I can't let you read through this, it's confidential, but I think we can outline yours from the components in this one."

Rebecca eyed the stack of papers and grumbled. "I'm going to have to allocate more money to the office supply budget." Despite feeling overwhelmed, she felt grateful that Laura had spoken up when she did. One week later, and they would have already missed the window to put their best foot forward.

Rebecca was writing out the list of items that needed to be in the board packets, and at the same time had a running list of carry-over items for the investor monthly reports. "Remind me again ... why did I agree to do monthly reporting?"

"I think you wanted the investors to trust you so they would give you even more money later."

"No. That's nice and all, but it wasn't that I wanted more money. It was that I was grateful for them to trust me with their money in the first place. I want them to see it is going to good use."

"Yes. And then they will trust you with more."

Rebecca turned and playfully threw a dry eraser at Don. She was relieved when he laughed. Apparently somewhere in the crazy hours, they had crossed the boundary between formal colleagues and working friendship.

"In seriousness though, I think you've got it all on your list there. Anything else you think to include is going to be icing on the glazed donut. At some point you've got to draw the line."

Rebecca made a mental note to double-check this advice with Liz. She trusted Don, but a second opinion was always welcome, especially when you were swimming as far out of your comfort zone as she was right now.

She snapped a quick picture of her whiteboard so she could work on the project at home this evening.

"Hi, Liz!"

The video chat connected a few seconds later, and like a doofus, Rebecca repeated her greeting.

"Rebecca! You have no idea how happy I was to hear from you. I kept thinking about you and not having time to reach out."

"All good things, I hope."

"Of course. But I think I already know your news. Small world and all that."

"Oh! Do tell. I love to know what the rumor mill has to say about me." Rebecca steepled her fingers and tapped them together like a children's cartoon villain.

"Is it true that you quit your high-powered nine-to-five and made a big bet on your own company?"

"Yes, this is true and accurate."

"Good for you! I know that couldn't have been easy. But I've got to know … Did you tell that boss of yours where to go on the way out?"

"I wish! She's actually one of my biggest contracting clients, so I'm not quite clear of her yet. Playing nice and all of that. What else have you heard?"

"That you have a solid concept and are out of beta in record time. And …

raising money already?"

"Oh yes, I raised my first-round last month. It was super awkward to ask people for money to support my own company, but I managed to reach my initial funding goal."

"I heard! A friend of mine is one of your investors. Which makes me wonder, why didn't you ask me?"

Rebecca felt herself blushing. "Honestly, I didn't ask any friends or family. I wanted investors based on the merit of the company."

"And now that you've proved yourself to yourself?"

"Sure, I'd be happy to send you an investor packet – thank you so much for considering Branches ..."

"But?"

"But that's not what I was calling for. Well, sort of not. I know you do a lot of investing and sit on a few boards. And I have my first board of director meeting coming up in two weeks and investor packets that need to go out, and I haven't really even seen one yet. I have a competent fractional CFO, but I'd love a second opinion I can trust on all of this."

"Oh, yeah. All of this is daunting until you find a routine, and then it'll just be part of your routine. And I get some terrible packets that are just sloppy. You definitely don't want to be doing that. When is your meeting?"

"Two weeks from yesterday."

"So, your board packets need to go out in six days, so they have them one week before the meeting."

Rebecca choked. "Six days?"

"You can do this. I'll send you a sample of one of the packets that I love and a sloppy packet for comparison. I'll redact anything you're not allowed to see – but as long as your books are in order, the biggest chunk of this will be creating templates and verbiage to follow for future packets."

"Liz to the rescue! I really appreciate this."

"Of course, I'm so glad that you thought to ask."

They visited for another half an hour before signing off. Rebecca left the call with a strange mix of relief and anxiety. The potential of networking continued to astound her, and she was starting to keep a tab of the people she felt she needed to reciprocate such support.

Rebecca wondered if she needed to breathe into a paper bag, like they did on 80s sitcoms when people were having funny-haha panic attacks. This felt awful. *My company is in financial peril! Grab a lunch sack and cue the laugh track.*

They were way off projections, and she needed to triple check the final numbers, but it looked like they were only pennies into the black this month. Rebecca felt a throbbing in her temple.

Her blooming headache was probably not helped by all the teenage TV volume she could hear through her home office wall. She poked her head in as she walked to the kitchen. "Mind turning that down?"

Tori didn't even look around. Her hand found the remote and pointed it at the tv and bopped the volume down a few decibels.

"A little more?"

Sigh. A few more bops.

"Thank you."

Tori was obviously still struggling with the belt tightening that was happening around the house. Richard had not won a prize at the poker tournament and had grudgingly agreed to let the country club go. This had ended some of their social lives, and inadvertently cut Tori off from some friends and activities as well.

TV therapy was all well and good, but Tori was going to be mad when

Rebecca cut the channel package this coming month as well. And she was going to need to. They were going to have to cancel the family vacation as well, and that was news no one was going to take well.

The company books were … terrifying. She wondered why no one told her to get a giant bottle of anti-anxiety meds when she started the company. Rebecca cracked a smile at herself. Yes, she should create a starter kit for prospective entrepreneurs. Inside she'd have instructions on how NOT to create projections for perspective investors and a giant bottle of Xanax.

She poured herself a glass of water and swallowed a generous helping of aspirin.

The first board of director meeting was nine days away. The packets were going out tomorrow. She squirmed internally. It was beyond embarrassing to be this far off her projections in month one. Basically, everything was taking twice as long and costing twice as much as she had projected. How was she ever going to catch up to her projections? Or was she at the top of a downward spiral taking her further and further away from her projections?

When she was in the corporate world, she had not appreciated how easy it was to throw money at these kinds of problems. Not hitting the deadline? Hire more contractors! With the exception of Lindsey, just about every manager she worked with had utilized money as the lever to solve whatever problem was hampering a project. Lindsey would cut people, projects, and perks.

She couldn't cut projects, her product was her product, and the for-hire contract work was her cash flow. She couldn't cut staff, as there was too much work as it was. She could cut the take-out meals, but then her programmers would walk, because they loved the perk. At the moment, the sales cycle took ages, the projects were overdue, and the money was short.

I'm vapor locking.

Wow. That was a term she hadn't thought of in years – when her dad would help her change her oil and replace her sparkplugs. He'd never do it for her, he'd make her put in her fair share of elbow grease. And while they worked, he'd talk about cars, about ignition sequences, and drive shafts. Backfires and vapor locks. Dad loved his car, and he loved his girl, and he'd show love to one by talking about the other.

A vapor lock was complicated, and she didn't remember exactly how it happened, but she remembered the result. The engine just stopped and wouldn't start again. You'd end up sitting on the side of the road banging on the steering wheel.

So, if her company was an engine about to lock up, what would she be able to do to fix it?

New fuel. New cash flow. A new product?

Hm. It would have to be a product that would be cheap to make and be sellable to existing clientele. Like an add-on?

Rebecca hurried back to her office and spent ten minutes brainstorming what an extra product might look like. At the end of it, she had a possible product but, she had to admit, she also had a great distraction. Something to make her feel slightly more hopeful about her business, but nothing that would help her current dilemma.

She shoved the document under a stack of papers and refocused on the task at hand. How to present a dismal business report to a fresh batch of investors.

Well, what is the good news?

Rebecca sat down and made a list. There had been some progress with the sales process, leads were up, meetings were happening. On the staffing side, they were able to bring in a new contractor that was extremely efficient at coding and problem solving. Liz had committed to investing $25K.

So, if she was honest, there was red ink, yes. But there were also pieces in place to grow. She could do this.

And Rebecca buckled down to writing her meeting agenda.

Chapter Eleven

"VOILA!" LAURA OPENED THE DOOR with a flourish to reveal a high-end conference room complete with polished table, overstuffed leather chairs and coffee on the sideboard.

Rebecca whistled in appreciation. "You're officially in charge of this for all time, you know that, right?"

"Yes!" Laura had sweet-talked the building management into letting Branches use this conference room free of charge. Rebecca had to admire her people skills.

Rebecca walked around the table, checking the AV set up and available power outlets. "Did you have a set up in mind?"

"Set up?"

"Yeah, like 'Rebecca sits here, presentation is done here.' That kind of stuff."

"Oh, definitely! I was going to even write up place cards for every seat, but I thought that might be overstepping."

"Well, yeah, good call on that. It isn't a wedding. But it definitely feels like an awkward Thanksgiving dinner. So, walk me through what you were picturing."

Sure enough, Laura had scoped out the best place to run the meeting from, which screen to use for presentations and how to connect her computer to the system.

Life saver. Rebecca gave herself a gold star for having the right people doing the right jobs.

Twenty minutes later, the last of the board members were arriving. Don set up camp right next to her seat, and Travis (*so good to see Travis!*) took the vacant seat opposite. He was her proposal for the independent industry knowledgeable board member, and she expected the board would ratify him today.

The rest of the seats were taken by Louise, Arun, and Michael, who was one of the early "in- the-room" yeses. Rebecca and Travis officially rounded out the board. Don was not a voting member, nor was her attorney, Fritz, who wasn't present but would be on-call should they need to consult by phone.

The other investors had been issued invitations to observe, and Liz said she'd come for moral support, but then had texted that she was running late. It didn't appear that anyone else would be coming, and so Rebecca called the room to attention.

Ugh!

Rebecca's heart was going too fast, like she was about to take a leap into dark water. The words she had prepared flew away like startled birds. She glanced at her agenda and decided to start there. "So excited to welcome you to the first official board meeting of Branches – I hope everyone got their board packet we sent out last week? If not, we have extras here." She looked around to ensure that each member had one in their hands. "First of all, I want to be respectful of your time and stick with our ninety-minute agenda. If there are items we're not able to fully cover, let's schedule a short Zoom in the next few days."

Louise already had her packet on the table, and Michael produced one from his briefcase. "Super impressed by the way. Most companies new to this don't send them out early, and then the meeting takes a million times longer to review everything."

Rebecca smiled at Michael and silently thanked Liz for her guidance. And Don, he had a lot to do with that too. "If you're looking at the bottom line, we're scraping by right now. Sales projections were on for the month, but there were production delays and extra expenditures, so while revenue was healthy, our outflow was a little over exuberant. We did have a last-minute investor come in, which helped balance out the short fall."

"Speaking of ..." Liz had just slipped into the room.

"Thanks for coming, Liz." Rebecca did a brief introduction to the rest of the board and resumed her presentation. "Now, if there are any questions on the balance sheet for the month, let's discuss that now before we move on to projections and adjustment to the business plans."

There were no questions, as they were all savvy enough investors to understand the profit and loss sheet.

The projections were going to be the rough part of the meeting. Rebecca steeled herself for it and pushed on. *Nowhere to go, but through.*

Rebecca took a deep breath and explained the details of the missed projections. She purposefully stayed upbeat as she shared their new hire, a software engineer that would help keep them on schedule. His costs were covered by closing deals more quickly, without the delays they had been experiencing.

Rebecca was trying very hard not to apologize for where things were. The words kept trying to pop out of her mouth, even though she knew she hadn't done anything wrong. They invested their money in her, and she had invested it in the company.

Nothing had been lost (yet), but her inner voice was yammering away. She smothered an insane urge to ask the room if that little voice was a woman thing.

Don't crack up at the first meeting, Rebecca.

She rallied as she wrapped her prepared talk. "So, you can see we had some unexpected things happen this month. And frankly, I don't want this to be a trend. Branches has the potential to be a great company, and our sales show that we have solutions to real problems. We're learning from our mistakes, and rarely are we repeating the same ones. But there's also a great amount of knowledge in this room. I'm hoping to tap into that experience, so Branches doesn't have to learn from the school of hard knocks indefinitely. I'd like to kick this next part of the agenda off with a discussion about future projections and making sure they are stretching for growth, yet achievable."

Arun shut his packet and picked it up to tap it on the table, as if they were a mess of paper to be beat into order. It was a strange move, considering the packet was bound neatly together, but it had the desired effect of drawing all the attention in the room. "I have to say, I am disappointed. It's not a good sign when you miss your numbers this badly in the first month. I don't invest to lose my money and looking at these books, it feels like I threw money in a black hole."

Ouch.

Rebecca had run several scenarios through her head leading up to this meeting, but none quite as blunt and, well, mean as this one. Luckily, before the silence could hang or Rebecca did something terrible like apologize to Arun, Michael chimed in.

"Let's not be too harsh here. A few missed numbers happen and making hasty short-term judgments will not improve the situation. Building a company is a marathon, not a sprint and I think everyone in this room knows that first-hand. Even if ..." A pointed look was directed toward Arun. "Some of us haven't experienced the ups and downs as recently as others." Michael paused, obviously to see if Arun was going to argue the point. After a beat of silence, he continued, "So keeping with that theme, I think we should consider adding more 'mile markers' to these projections. Mile markers were how we termed it with my first business, by the way. We found that they helped us identify problems sooner. And when you're in a building phase, like Branches is now, knowing issues sooner is always better because then there is a chance to fix the issue."

"We called them 'building blocks,'" Louise offered. "Probably because we were an education-based service. But the same idea."

"Oh, I like that," Michael said. "Mile markers can sound like micromanaging. Hmm, building blocks. That's clever. I'm going to steal that and use it at all of my board meetings."

"You're welcome to it." Louise was smiling.

Rebecca was a little bewildered at this burgeoning friendship, but Arun just rolled his eyes. "Alright, we're going to measure more things, lots of little things. And what are these numbers going to tell us?"

"Well, Rebecca," Michael said, "I noticed that the projections are missing some details on the sales side. What is your lead pipeline like? Enterprise sales are nice and big infusions of cash, but they also take a long time to close. We could be measuring the number of new leads coming in and the average sales cycle. From there, we can monitor the new leads volume and try to improve them, and on the other side, try to shorten the sales cycle."

Rebecca nodded; what he said made sense, and why hadn't she thought of this?

Michael continued, "But as a building block, what you measure matters.

This seems key when it comes to leads, because a significant drop off identified and resolved now, will prevent a disastrous cash flow problem six months from now."

"You're right. And actually, the timing on this is perfect." Rebecca pulled out a sheet of paper and started taking notes on the blank side. "So far, the leads have been coming from my own contacts and leads we collected at a tradeshow. Our website is up, but there's not much traffic going to it yet. There's another tradeshow coming up in a few months, but it's likely that one of our main competitors will be there throwing around a lot of money again."

"Which one?" Louise asked.

"Octopus. The last tradeshow we were at, they threw a huge party. Open bar and lots of giant purple inflatable tentacles everywhere," Rebecca advised.

"Hm. Okay, before we dive into conference optimization strategies, are you sure this is a space you want to compete in?" Michael asked.

"I think I have to. Otherwise, I'll eventually run out of contacts in my 'rolodex.' And companies who don't know me personally will need the legitimacy of running into us at these kinds of things."

"I might want to challenge that assumption later, but for the moment, let's go over lead-generation strategies," Michael said.

Rebecca leaned in with interest.

"I thought we were going to get more measurements, immediately," Arun broke in. "Why are we wasting everyone's time talking about marketing? We should be setting these mile markers."

Everyone paused to look at Arun. He seemed to squirm under their collective scrutiny.

This negativity was not the answer, and Rebecca was going to have to do something about it. She smiled at him. "Thanks for keeping the meeting on track, Arun. Michael, I'd love to exchange thoughts and strategies with you about our upcoming lead generation. I'll have Laura set up a meeting for next week. Would that work for you?"

Michael gave her a warm smile. "Absolutely."

Don, who had said very little so far in the meeting, jumped in. Rebecca belatedly realized that he had been quickly typing away on his laptop for the last few minutes. He had connected it to the main screen and shared a document for everyone to see. "This is a dashboard that I have seen used with other companies. I think it can be easily adapted to fit Branches."

Rebecca was impressed. At first glance, it seemed all the major metrics were included.

"This can be updated on a weekly basis. Rebecca, I'll have to coordinate with your team to collect the data, but I think we can create some automations around some of it, so it won't create a time burden."

"Oh, this is genius, Don, thank you."

Arun grumped and added a few more metrics to the list, but in the end, the board adopted it, and Rebecca felt like she could breathe again.

The meeting adjourned with fifteen minutes to spare. Rebecca wanted nothing more than to call Richard and ask him to meet her at their favorite bar. But instead, she leaned over and asked Arun if he could stay for a minute.

"I don't see why."

Rebecca continued to smile and make eye contact with him.

"But I guess I have a few minutes."

She thanked and said goodbye to the rest of the team. Liz gave her a wink and a thumbs up as she left. That left Arun and Rebecca a little bit of privacy so they could have a frank conversation.

"So, Arun, I want to start by saying that I appreciate that you invested in Branches. I know why I decided I want to work with you. But after this meeting, I feel like I need to ask: why did you decide to invest in Branches?

Arun blinked in surprise. "I like enterprise software. There's good money in it, good returns."

"That makes sense, but there's a lot of companies in the space. Why did you pick Branches?"

"Well, I think you're smart. The product you're making has a market, and I think you can pull off a win for me."

Rebecca nodded, considering this. "Thank you. I appreciate that you believe in me, but after the meeting we just had, I'd have never known you felt that way. At all. It seemed like nothing anyone said in here was ever good enough. In fact, you seemed angry."

Arun actually laughed.

Rebecca felt slightly dislocated; this was not the reaction she was expecting.

"I always do this. I don't want to get too close to the entrepreneurs I invest in. You all do better if I can keep you at arm's length. You hyper-competitive types need to keep on your toes, so I question everything you do."

Rebecca took a steadying breath. There was so much wrong with what he'd just said, so many assumptions. But what would help her most now? "I think that I may be a little bit different than the typical entrepreneur that you've worked with in the past," Rebecca said diplomatically. "I really embrace and work well with constructive criticism. I'm actively seeking out advice and ideas from the board on how to grow Branches and do better. In the room today, your feedback was coming across as negativity, which makes it not only hard to hear and act on, but it also made it difficult for the rest of the board to contribute as well." She paused to allow him time to let it sink in. "I feel like you have a lot to contribute, and a lot of great ideas. I want you to be a valuable member of the board. But to do that, I'm going to need you to be constructive in your participation."

Arun sat up. "Well, you're the first female CEO I have invested in. I didn't realize that women were this much more sensitive than men. But this is how I manage my investments; it's how I've always done it."

Rebecca leaned back in her chair so she wouldn't scream in his face. She was amazed at how even her voice was when she said, "I am the CEO of Branches, and I happen to be a woman. I think the difference here is not sensitivity but being open and honest. I've told you what works best for Branches, and the tone and culture I'm building here. I feel confident we can find our way, as long as we respect each other."

Before Arun could bluster a reply, there was a knock on the door. Rebecca answered to find an overloaded secretary ready to set up for the next group using the room.

A few moments later, Rebecca shook Arun's hand in the hallway. "Thanks for your time. I look forward to working with you."

"Me too." He was smiling again.

Who knew?

Rebecca ducked into the washroom down the hall from the conference room. No one was around, so she took the moment to give herself a good-long look in the mirror as she washed her hands. All the strain she had felt leading into that meeting seemed to have melted away. The majority of the board had been supportive, and she had confronted Arun head-on and … survived?

She gave herself a smile in the mirror. She might have a stress-relieving cry about all this later, but for the moment, it felt good to smile again. She was determined to try and smile the rest of the day.

Popping back into the hallway, she found Travis pinned awkwardly in the hallway by Arun. She felt her smile melt into a quizzical frown. Travis looked up and caught her frown. He winked.

Relaxing slightly, Rebecca gestured upward towards the office on a higher floor. He gave her a slight nod. Rebecca practically tiptoed down the hallway to avoid attracting Arun's attention. Travis would have flagged her if he needed her.

———————

Upstairs, things were the calm, controlled chaos of a rapidly growing company. Lunch trays had been delivered and devoured, and the programmers were back at their desks snacking, typing, and occasionally cracking jokes. The jokes were key with her team. If problems were brewing, the silence would become thick and impenetrable.

Rebecca admired the scene for a moment. She had built this. And she would continue to build it.

Back in her office, she had just slipped into her email inbox when Travis ducked into her office. He leaned his back against the door and stood there for a moment, clearly gathering himself. She watched up with amazement as he slowly dissolved from a playful smile to uncontrolled giggling.

"Uh. You okay there, Travis?"

"That guy. Is such. A trip!" Travis was wiping tears from his eyes and gasping for air.

"Arun? What did he say?"

"Well, it started with a good grilling about the financial particulars of me being here."

Rebecca felt her eyebrows quirk up as she tried to imagine what the heck Arun had asked. "Like was I paying you to attend the meeting and be on the board?"

"Sort of. Who paid for my flight, hotel, meals, all that."

"He was right there when we voted you onto the board today. How did he miss that?" Rebecca queried.

"I think that's what set him off, actually. Who was I, why was I an 'expert,' what was I contributing that was so valuable."

Rebecca was still at a loss.

"Rebecca … He thought …" Travis gulped more air, trying to control his laughter. "He thought I was your boy toy." Travis met her eyes, his body twitching with the strain of withholding his laughter. And then he dissolved again into giggles.

Rebecca felt herself get very still. She was torn between shock that Travis had been questioned like this and anger at Arun for even thinking of it. Her body seemed locked between laughing and running down to the lobby and cheerfully beating Arun to death with her high heel.

"Apparently men and women are *not* just friends, and who do we think we're fooling? No man would use his Frequent Flyer miles for a little company like this unless he had another reason."

"That little troll," Rebecca said with a forced smile. "I think I might be about to commit murder. Yes. This is murder in my heart. Stand back, I have a high heel, and I'm not afraid to use it."

Travis quickly locked the door and resumed his post against it. "Don't you dare. I told him we were both happily married to other people." Travis cocked his head. "I didn't show him the pictures of my family, though. I didn't want to protest too much." He snorted.

"I think I need to kick him off the board. I know he's the biggest investor, but I don't think it's going to be worth it. He's awful, I basically did the whole manager 'why do you want to work here' subtext, 'don't you want to quit' routine with him after the board meeting. And he walks out and doubles down? Who does that?"

"No," Travis said adamantly. "Let the troll be the little troll that he is. He's someone who is always going to be convinced the waiter spit in his food. We have years of free entertainment ahead of us."

Rebecca looked Travis in the eye. "I'm so sorry he said that to you."

"It's okay. You should take it as a compliment. Smelt it, dealt it rules – the guy has a crush on you."

Travis then broke into another peel of laughter.

Rebecca did take off her shoe and throw it this time. "Take it back! I think I might have to go power wash my brain after this."

Chapter Twelve

TORI FAILED TO RETURN THE serve. She could have gotten it, as Rebecca had seen her field similar serves repeatedly. But this time, the ball sailed right under her racket.

Rebecca winced in sympathy. Tori was clearly getting frustrated. It was the first match since her private lessons stopped. Rebecca was shocked that her skills were already getting rusty. Or maybe Tori was just getting in her own head now? She would occasionally get wrapped up in past serves that she'd fail to play the current one.

The coaches would always help her get straightened out. But this time?

RICHARD: *How is it going?*

> *I've got to find a way to get her lessons again.*

RICHARD: *That bad?*

> **She's just lost a lot of confidence (I think).**

Rebecca snapped a ten-second video of their daughter and sent it to Richard.

RICHARD: *Yeah, she's pulling. And … I know I'm not supposed to say anything … But is she gaining weight?*

Rebecca looked up in surprise. Was Tori gaining weight? She knew that Tori was unhappy and not going out with her friends quite as much. It had been a blow to her social life when they had left the country club. And cut her allowance.

Rebecca had noticed her own weight gain but had written it off to stress. But maybe it was not just her feeling the pressure.

> **You might be right. But don't you dare mention it to her.**

Richard replied with the three monkey icons—see no evil, hear no evil, speak no evil.

———

The next day, Rebecca couldn't stop thinking about Tori. It wasn't fair that she was suffering because Rebecca had decided to start a company. Rebecca felt horrible, and the only way she could see to fix it was to bring in more cashflow for the company, stat.

A few weeks ago, she had had an idea for a new product. What had she done with it?

When she got home from the tennis match, she pored through her notes but only found some cryptic notes and a reminder to call Melanie, the marketing consultant.

But a quick search of her phone showed she hadn't called Melanie. But ... she would call Melanie if she had an idea that would need marketing. With that in mind, she texted Melanie.

MELANIE THE MARVELOUS: *We finally doing drinks?*

> **We did drinks like 2 weeks ago.**

MELANIE THE MARVELOUS: *And? 2 weeks feels like 2 decades. Must drink.*

> **I was thinking something a little more focused. Meet me at the office?**

MELANIE THE MARVELOUS: *Boo.*

> **I'll buy a giant bag of caramels ...**

MELANIE THE MARVELOUS: *Kryptonite! You have found my weakness ...*

> **Well, you did tell me, "I run on coffee and caramels," so I'll have a caramel macchiato waiting for you too.**

MELANIE THE MARVELOUS: *Alright, I'm convinced. Tell me when.*

Rebecca triumphantly wrapped up the details. She couldn't technically afford Melanie's rates, but she could bribe her with coffee and sugar and see what her magnificent brain could pump out in an afternoon. In the meantime, she started a primer list to get the conversation going.

———————

Not too many days later, Melanie showed up at her office door. Rebecca was prepared with a variety of caramels and a giant steaming caramel macchiato from the local coffee shop, as promised.

Melanie deftly unwrapped a caramel and popped it into her mouth with a satisfied smile. "Okay, you've got me here. And I'm here for as long as the caramels hold out. So, what's up?"

"Well, long story short, I have a cashflow problem. My current sales cycle is long, and programmers are expensive. So, I need a simple new product, something to sell to the same marketplace, same clients, that is just a no-brainer add-on. It needs to be light on set up, use the tech we already have, the people we already have, and be of enough value that people buy it on the spot."

"Hmm. So, something easy to make, easy to deliver and targeted at your existing marketplace?"

"Yeah."

"Honey, no offense. But I have no idea what you do here." Melanie gave her a broad grin and a shrug. "I mean, it looks impressive, and you're definitely doing something, but I have no idea what it is."

"Oh. Well, in a nutshell, think of a business with lots of transactions —banks, credit cards, airlines, major retail stores? They have a ton of reconciliation that needs to happen every night. The infrastructure that they're using is out of date, and the people who spoke that code are retiring. So, I'm reinventing the wheel, bringing it up to date, and creating a secure reconciliation process with a ton of computing power."

"Geez. I had no idea."

"Yeah, it's not the kind of product that will ever have a Super Bowl commercial."

"No kidding, but it's like the kind of technology that makes the world go round."

"Yeah. I'm not the only one jumping into this space. There's competition. But there's more demand now than ever, and the old tech is barely able to keep up with the current technology."

"Are you selling one-off products or subscription?"

"Right now, one-off until Branches is more stable and establishes a solid performance track record. Then, yes, the plan is to move to a subscription-based service with pricing dependent on the number of transactions."

"For now, you're stuck with making individual sales to large corporations. What is your sales cycle and process looking like?"

"Long." Rebecca gave a rueful sigh. "I had a big rolodex going into this, and I'm still working my way through it. Basically, I'm the sales department, and I don't think I can shorten the sales cycle, and I don't think I can bring someone in to do it for me."

"Rolodex," Melanie repeated.

"Contact list, whatever."

Melanie winked and popped another caramel into her mouth. "Alright, so subscription is out. You aren't going to bring on another sales rep, so it must be something that you can reach out to your existing relationships about. Is this new product supposed to be a lead magnet into your larger product sales funnel?"

"Depends. I'd like it to be a complimentary product, so something I can offer existing clients or potential ones. If one leverages into the other, that's fine, but I'd like to dip into the open wallets I already have, you know what I mean."

"Yup. So, here's what I'm thinking …" And she was off to the races.

The rest of the afternoon was filled with laughter, sugar highs and silly ideas. Finally, they landed on a solid idea: a course. It would teach Agile Development specific to transactional management. They were going to call it "Technically New Thinking" and brand it with a little stick of a cartoonish Wille E. Coyote TNT dynamite. There were still three caramels left in the bag when they wrapped up the session.

Rodney's weekly check-in wrapped up on a positive note. He was rightly skeptical of the Technically New Thinking course – or TNT, as they were now calling it – but it would require very little from his department. It wouldn't throw off his current schedule, so they were both happy. As he opened the door to leave, Rebecca caught a glimpse of Laura lingering outside.

Laura seemed nervous, hovering but not quite taking the initiative to walk in. Rebecca wondered what was up. She gestured Laura in with a smile.

"I know you're super busy, and I'm not on the schedule right now."

"Since when do you need an appointment; my door is always open to you. What's going on? Rebecca gestured to the open seat in front of her desk. "Is everything okay with you?"

"Oh!" Laura started in surprise. "Yes, I'm fine. What I wanted to talk to you about is you."

"Me?"

"Yes, I see how busy you are, and I've been trying to figure out how I can help you more." Laura looked up at her, seeming nervous. When Rebecca smiled, Laura kept going with a little more confidence. "You're always strapped for time, and there are things on your plate that I could do to free up your time. I did some research, and it isn't unusual for assistants to take over their boss' email or have their phone number diverted to the assistant in the company directory. Or handle the creation of the marketing collateral. There's a lot of steps there that are just going back and forth that aren't a good use of your time."

"Huh." Rebecca sat back in her chair. She thought she'd been handing things off to Laura, but Laura clearly felt she could be contributing more. "Well …" Rebecca wasn't sure what she was willing to let go of. Instead of rattling off a quick, haphazard list, she decided to take a different tact. "I think you're right. I should be moving things off my plate. And, frankly, I'm not ready to let go of my phone and email just yet, mainly because I really hate it when I don't hear back from the person I wrote to or called, and then their assistant returns the call. It feels like they think they're too good to do the core things. Make sense?" Rebecca saw Laura deflate a bit. "But … I think you've got your own set of skills that we can be utilizing better. So, what else would you like to do, or think would be a helpful contribution?"

"The monthly newsletter. You procrastinate on it every month. I could totally take that."

"It is official, Laura, you are the best. *YES.* Please take that, I'd be happy to never see it again." Rebecca considered for a moment. "But always know you can come to me with questions or problems. I promise I won't take this red-headed stepchild back, but I'm available to be your sounding board."

"No take-backs, got it." Laura made a note on her pad and then looked up expectantly.

Rebecca smiled to herself. *Okay, game on. Let's see if we can fill the page.*

In the end, Rebecca handed over all logistics for the upcoming conference, monthly newsletters, contractor updates, let Laura start a YouTube channel to promote the functionality of Branches and gave her the beginning three steps to TNT, researching course platforms, finding a technical writer to write the content of the course, and creating a brand package for the website. No small ask, but Laura seemed to relish the idea of the project.

Laura left the room standing a little taller, and Rebecca smiled as she gently shut the door. Laura may be still in college, but she was going places.

Rebecca made it a practice to give her team her undivided attention. Her theory was if she cared about them, they would care about their jobs more. That said, her cellphone had been neglected on her desk over the course of her two back-to-back meetings. It silently buzzed the desktop for the umpteenth time. She scooped it up to check what was shaking.

A message from Tori: school apparently was the worst (again). A message from Richard: his flight was running late (again). And a missed call from Travis. Plus, a text message that read: *Left you a voicemail. It's important!*

The voicemail was a breathless Travis. "Octopus just closed a huge round of funding, Rebecca. Part of the raise was predicated on them closing a deal with Bank of America, which means they have Merrill Lynch and their foot in the door on Wall Street. They're also talking about an initial public offering, a damn IPO, within five years."

Chapter Thirteen

REBECCA WAS IN A ROTTEN mood when she got home that night. After viciously filling the dishwasher and banging around for a bit in the laundry room, Richard cornered her while she ruthlessly purged her closet.

"What is going on?" he asked.

"Nothing." Rebecca tossed a t-shirt in the donate pile. She could tell Richard was giving her an "I don't believe you look," so she busied herself pulling out more hangers of clothes to sort.

"Whatever it is, you can talk to me about it."

"I know."

The silence stretched. She pitched a dress into the donate pile.

"Don't get rid of that one."

"Why not?"

"Because you love it. You wear it whenever you want to feel special."

Rebecca stopped, considering the dress. "I can't see wearing it again. It just doesn't feel possible."

"What isn't possible?"

"Going out to a fancy dinner. Going to a show. Having reasons to celebrate. I ..." Suddenly, Rebecca couldn't speak anymore. She was choking up, the tears that had been threatening since Travis' voicemail were starting to pour over.

"Oh, honey." Richard gently pulled the dress from her hands and hung it carefully back in the closet. He wrapped her in a supportive hug and just stood there as Rebecca stifled a sob into his shoulder. "We're going to get through this tough time, together. And there's going to be fancy dinners and anniversaries and graduations and lots of good things to look forward to."

He held her a little tighter and Rebecca let all the tension go, feeling her body relax into his.

"This is just a moment, that's all."

They were silent for a while. When Rebecca felt calmer, she gave him a squeeze and he let her go. She rubbed her eyes and was a bit embarrassed by the wet splotch on his t-shirt.

"Feel better?"

"Yeah."

"Want to talk about it?"

"Oh, I think it's a lot of things. But the final straw today was an Octopus update."

"Uh-oh. Did they steal your best client?"

"No, but they closed a huge banking deal. Which means that they now have validation and visibility in the financial sector. They will likely IPO in less than five years and be a household name in six."

Richard's eyebrows dipped in confusion. "I thought you weren't going after the financial sector because it has a really high security bar, and it would bankrupt the company to invest that much this early."

"It's true. But I always envisioned we'd get there eventually."

"So, these guys have either spent a lot of resources to comply with all the required standards, or they're frantically building the infrastructure now."

"True. They must have had something working to be able to sell it to the bank though. Maybe."

"Maybe. Maybe not. But this deal doesn't affect you at all, does it? Your market niche is health care and gas transactions, right?"

"Oil and gas, yeah."

"So really, this news means that your main competition has gotten their first major deal in a market segment you aren't competing in, and they likely are taking on a lot of regulations and expense to fulfill that contract."

Rebecca took a deep breath and let it out slowly. "I'm trying to figure out if you're right, and I'm overreacting, or if you're right and I'm overreacting.

"Not overreacting," Richard reassured her. "You're tired, you've put a lot into this, and it isn't always smooth sailing. But you have no idea what's going on in that other boat. And ..." He raised an eyebrow at her. "You always said this company is not a 'household name' product."

She smiled wanly. "It really isn't."

Rebecca decided that if she had the chance, she was going to change the use of the word "milestones" with the investors. It was an antiquated word that evoked wooden carts and uneducated populace on the Appian Road. It was long to spell, a mouthful to say and not nearly cool enough to express the ambition it represented.

She would replace milestones with high jumps or planetary launches … just as soon as she could hit a milestone on time. Until then, changing terms would be like rearranging the furniture on the deck of the Titanic. And right now, she was two clients short of achieving her milestone.

It was time to shake some bushes and see what flew out.

The list she had compiled was actually two columns. The first half of the list were people she knew well and who might be willing to introduce her to contacts at target companies. The second column was a list of companies they seemed well connected to via LinkedIn. The goal was for her contact to either introduce her and Branches or vouch for her if talks were already in progress with these target companies.

The introduction would cut a lot of red tape. But she was also hoping that if sales stalled out, her contact would be able to help suss out the source of the objection. She doubted it would be anything so simple as cost. If it was, she would have printed up coupons months ago. No, the issue was likely the risk of change. It was a big step to transition from one scheduling system to another. And the cost of getting it wrong could be detrimental for their companies. So how would they decide to take the chance?

Jeremy answered on the second ring. His voice sounded crystal clear, even though he was on the other side of the planet. "Hey, Rebecca! What's shakin'?" Although Jeremy had already quit his corporate career before Rebecca ever had the idea to start Branches, he stayed in contact with the Airport Squad. And this tribe had become her de facto unofficial advisory board long before she started raising money and having a true board of directors.

After a few minutes of small talk (he was currently biking his way across Vietnam), they got down to business.

"I'm getting some early adopters, having some success with the bucket of contacts I had when I started. Now I'm going to be pivoting to companies where I don't have pre-existing relationships. And before I dive in, I wanted to get your insight on how corporations go about buying new technology."

There was silence on the line. Rebecca schooled herself to wait.

"Wow, that's a big question. But I guess I'd like to know: why are you asking me?" Jeremy queried.

"Well, I think you've got some distance from the industry. Enough to reflect back, objectively."

"True. True." He then went silent again.

"And of course, I respect your opinion." Rebecca winced. She should have waited.

"Thanks. I appreciate that. And I'm not sure what I know that you don't already know. So yeah, there might be some 'well duhs' in this list."

Rebecca was ready for all and any advice.

Jeremy went on, "FOMO – fear of missing out – is a big one. If you're able to build a buzz, companies are going to come to you, and close a lot faster. And until you can attract companies to you rather than go to them, the best thing you can do is have glowing testimonials. You'll need testimonials either way."

"I've got some," Rebecca replied proudly.

"However many you have, get more, with specifics about how your product improved their company or their personal lives."

Rebecca grimaced a little. "Okay."

"Another big one is timing. There's always going to be internal pressure and conversations that you don't know about. But I'd subscribe to all the job sites for openings similar to where Branches could be utilized. Then get intros to the VP or CEO," Jeremy suggested.

"Oh! I hadn't thought of that one."

"I had success with that strategy right when LinkedIn took off. I had just started my first big sales job. And I'd watch the alerts, then leverage my network to get the introduction I needed."

Rebecca was impressed. "That's smart."

"Thank you! It helped me get to bike through humid pieces of paradise like this."

"Oh, is that my hint that I should let you go?" Rebecca asked with a laugh.

"No, I'm not currently sitting on my bike! But there's a really tempting bar down the block. When we're done, I'm going to walk over there and order something cold and filled with alcohol."

Have one for me. "Okay, I'll try to get through the rest of my questions quickly then. I have a list of prospect companies I think Branches would be a good fit for. Can I rattle off a few names, and if one is a good fit or you have a good relationship with them, would you be open to giving introductions?"

"Sure, if one's a good fit, I'd be happy to introduce you," Jeremy replied.

Rebecca started rattling off names until Jeremy interrupted with, "Go back, did you say Hyadon?"

"Yeah."

"Remember Marissa?" Jeremy asked. "She was the director over at C2H for ages. She just moved over to Hyadon – some kind of VP position."

"Really? I don't remember her. Would you feel comfortable doing intros?" Rebecca crossed her fingers.

"Heck yeah. As a new VP, I'm sure she's looking for some way to make her mark."

"Awesome. Anything I should know about what makes her tick?"

Jeremy was silent for a moment. "Get a one-sheet together of your testimonials and get it designed to stand out in the proposal."

Rebecca jotted it down on her notepad.

"Okay, let's hear the rest of the list."

Twenty minutes later, Rebecca had a promise from Jeremy to introduce her to three contacts at target companies. Before she rang off, she had to ask though, "Do you miss it? The corporate world?"

"Honestly, sometimes I do, usually when I'm out of my element meeting new people. It's really easy to define yourself to strangers by what you do. It was a bit to get used to introducing myself as someone biking around tropical destinations."

"You miss the corporate flex." Rebecca smiled.

"Yeah, I miss the way people looked impressed. But the work itself? The endless to-do list? Nah. It's actually been really good for me to learn who I am without a boss and a deadline."

Rebecca took advantage of a gap in time zones to go for a walk after the call with Jeremy. Try as she might, she couldn't help but feel she had identified the exact same problem Jeremy had. And had gone in completely the other direction. She was the boss, sure, but now she had a board looking over her shoulder, and more deadlines and responsibilities than she could ever possibly meet. While she had no particular dream to bike around Southeast Asia, she did have to acknowledge the appeal. No agenda to achieve, no payroll to sweat.

No matter how she tried, it didn't seem possible to put down the responsibilities of Branches. So, when she made it around the block, she went back upstairs to call California.

————

Three calls later, she hit pay-dirt. Sarah, from her Airport Squad, had apparently been keeping close tabs on the talks between Branches and one of the companies Rebecca had been in talks with. The talks had stalled out because converting their current system was going to be disruptive, and they weren't convinced that Branches was going to "last" as a company – that they would have to switch again if Branches went under.

"Yikes."

"Yeah, I didn't know what to say."

"I totally get it. I own the company and will need a moment to strategize. Maybe I should send out a special invitation to celebrate closing our first round of funding and offer free updates or 'priority support' levels."

"Hmm. Honestly, unless you raised millions in the round, I think it would undermine you. But priority support is awesome, especially since it doesn't really cost you more, but big companies definitely hate being put on hold when something goes wrong."

"Excellent point. I bet I could get worldwide coverage put together fairly easily too."

"I've got a contact that might be able to help you with that. He runs a support center in Bangladesh."

"Cool. Send it my way!" Internally, Rebecca wondered what it would cost, but if having "priority support" was the lever that closed more business, it would be completely worth it.

When they hung up, Rebecca had a plan of attack to land at least one company. And she would send the offer out to a few more select companies as well. It was great to have a new lever to use.

Overall, the evening had been a successful one. Four calls had yielded lots of advice, and the promise of nine new warm introductions – her "airport squad" was being so generous, donating their time and trusting her with their contacts. She wondered how she would ever be able to express how grateful she was. But now she needed to go home and see her neglected husband and child!

———

"Where did the pictures come from?" Rebecca asked Laura the next day.

"A royalty-free stock image website. I've cited all the images per terms and conditions, so I feel confident on that one."

Laura had presented her with a functional website for TNT. Rebecca was really impressed with how it looked. It was a sleek design, completely professional with a uniform-branded feel to it. There were gaps here and there where Laura hadn't had the copy to fill in spaces, but she'd be able to provide it. Rebecca made a note to review all of it to make sure the current copy hit all the sales points and didn't promise anything too off the wall.

"Excellent." Rebecca clicked around a bit more. "Do we have a lead magnet created yet?"

"It's at the designer, and I have the email campaign drafted too. I'll need your help with it, however. I want to make sure it is accurate."

Rebecca nodded. This was impressive. It would perform well ... if Rebecca could get enough time blocked off to actually create the content for the training. Then maybe peel off one of the programmers to whip it together for delivery. Maybe Jonathan.

She made a few more notes of next "to-dos" and thanked Laura for her hard work.

Laura gave a skeptical look to the full list on Rebecca's desk. "Anything there I can take for you?"

"Ugh." Rebecca scanned down the list. "Yeah, it's a bit unmanageable at the moment, isn't it." Her brain was quickly doing the arithmetic of priorities, what was a current priority versus what had been hanging out on the list so long it was becoming a priority. "Okay, I need you to contact our India counterparts and ask how much it would be to have five people doing stress testing on Branches for the next month."

"Alright."

"Organize the conference room for the next board meeting and send out invites to the major players."

"Got it."

"And when you order lunch, can you get me a side of fruit, fruit anything? I feel like I'm going to get beriberi if I don't take better care of myself."

Laura grinned. "I'll see what I can do."

———

"Absolutely not."

Rodney's reaction took Rebecca aback. She hadn't expected any resistance to throwing more work towards Jonathan in a moonlighting capacity.

"Wow. Okay. What's going on that I don't know about?"

Rodney looked slightly ashamed. "Sorry, I guess that was a little strong. But Jonathan's work has been sloppy lately. He's missing deadlines, and when he turns it in, it has bugs. He's leaving early and always looks like he is working on three hours of sleep. I don't want to jump to conclusions or seem like I'm tanking him, but I've seen these tale-tell signs before. With moonlighters."

"You think he's working for someone else?"

"Yes."

"How? My brain is fried when I'm done at the end of the day. How could he keep going for someone else?"

"Well, he can't. Not for long. That's why he's getting sloppy."

"Have you talked to him at all? To see if something else is going on?"

"I tried. I ribbed him that I hadn't seen anyone drink that much coffee since Larry's twins were born. He just grunted and went back to his desk."

Rebecca tried valiantly not to roll her eyes. Why would Rodney think teasing a man about his coffee addiction was a substitute for having a frank conversation about an employee's failing performance? She was going to have to take the reins here and teach Rodney by example.

"Okay, I'd like you to go back and document the most recent incidents of poor performance and send them to me by the end of day tomorrow. Then continue documentation. I'll review the first round of documentation and then set a date for you, Jonathan, and myself to discuss the issues."

"Are you planning on firing him?" Rodney asked. He couldn't seem to make eye contact with her.

"Without seeing the list, I can't say for sure. But the issue must be addressed quickly and directly. If he wants to keep his job, it will become obvious, quickly."

Rodney was nodding, still not quite looking at her.

"You did the right thing by telling me. I'll treat him fairly. But we're a small company with limited resources. Everyone has to pull their weight when the team is as lean as it is. It's always better to train and support team members rather than hire and train from scratch. But if he's no longer 'team Branches' and his shortfalls create problems for the team, it will get toxic and burn everyone out. Telling me ultimately protects the rest of the team."

Rodney finally looked her in the eyes. "Okay, thanks." He left a few moments later.

Rebecca looked at her to-do list. *TNT will have to wait for now.*

Chapter Fourteen

REBECCA LET HER COMPUTER BAG slip from her shoulder. She made sure it had a gentle landing, but that was about all the energy she had left in her body. She really just wanted to eat a solid meal full of carbs and slip beneath the sheets of her bed.

A hopeful sniff in the direction of the kitchen revealed nothing. *Was it my turn to cook? What day is it? Tuesday?* She didn't want to pull her phone out to check, but she had a sneaking suspicion that Richard was on a late flight back. "Tori? You home?"

Nothing. The house was quiet.

Maybe she could just go directly to bed. It seemed like far too much trouble to figure out what to eat. And where her family was. Rebecca wondered if that made her a bad person, but she was honestly too tired to figure it out.

In college, when her brain was incredibly taxed, she'd take a shower to give herself a moment to relax and not feel like she had to read, or write a paper, or do anything.

A shower, she decided, was exactly what she needed right now. And when that was done, if she put on clothes, she'd come back downstairs and figure things out. And if she put on pajamas, she'd just go to bed.

To her immense disappointment, she didn't even make it into the shower before the front door banged open.

"Mom! Dinner!"

Did everything just solve itself for me? That would be a change.

Rebecca scrambled back into her clothes and headed downstairs to investigate.

Richard and Tori were happily chattering and unboxing Chinese dishes in the kitchen. She noted with a smile that they had ordered all the family's favorites and were laying it out on the kitchen island exactly like she would have done.

"Smells delicious." Rebecca realized suddenly that she was ravenous.

"Tori's idea. She's a genius, our daughter."

Tori rolled her eyes but still looked pleased.

They filled their plates and settled around the dinner table. After the initial rush to eat had passed, conversation resumed.

"Our genius daughter also had another stroke of brilliance."

"Hm?" Rebecca said around a mouthful of mushu.

"We need a vacation."

Rebecca used the excuse to chew and swallow before responding. "We do?"

"We always go somewhere in the spring," Tori jumped in. "It's usually planned by now. So, I thought, let's make a plan and go."

"I'm not sure an extravagant vacation is in the cards this year."

Rebecca looked at Richard. Why was he making her be the bad guy here? He knew their financial situation just as well as she did.

"Nothing extravagant," Tori assured her. "I was thinking maybe a long weekend like we did when I was a kid. Remember that trip we took to that island with the beach?"

Rebecca squinted, attempting to remember anything like Tori was describing. "You mean the trip we took to Grand Cayman in the middle of the Caribbean?"

"That was the Caribbean? I thought that was somewhere close by. I don't remember going to the airport."

"You slept most of the way." Rebecca heard the chiding in her voice and inwardly cringed.

"Oh."

It was silent at the table.

Rebecca took another bite of her dinner and looked at Richard. *What is he doing?*

"Well, I do have an idea," Richard volunteered somewhat sheepishly. "In a couple of weeks, I have to be in Miami for a conference. We could use some of the miles we've racked up to fly you two down. Nice beaches, warm weather. What do you say?"

"Yes!" Tori chimed in.

Rebecca put her fork down. "I'm glad you two have this worked out, but I can't go. You should definitely go, but I just can't leave the office right now. The business is in too precarious of a place right now."

"Honey, you could take the weekend off."

"No, Richard, I can't." She hated how sharp her voice sounded. All her frustrations seemed to boil to the surface, and she tried to keep her stress and resentment in check. Really, how dare he tell her that she could take time off? What did he think he knew better than she did?

"What would happen?"

"I don't know, and that's a problem! I have my fingers in the dam on a million little things. And it changes all the time. I can't plan for what will be going on tomorrow, never mind weeks from now. If I walk away for a second, this whole thing could fall apart. I can't run off to Florida with you."

Tori was looking at her, shocked.

Rebecca took a breath and tried to get herself under control. For Tori. "Look. You two should go. You should have fun. I just. Can't."

"Honey ..."

"No." And with tears brimming, she got up and left. The shower was probably a good idea after all.

Rebecca felt her heart beating a little too quickly as she waited for Jonathan to arrive. She had thought through the conversation and how she wanted it to go, but she had to admit to herself that she was more emotional than she should be. She had talked with power players, brokered multi-million-dollar deals, and (unfortunately) had to let employees go. But this time was different. Jonathan may be stepping out on Branches, and it felt weirdly personal, like he was cheating on her.

Rodney shuffled through the door half a step before Jonathan. He gave her a small supportive smile. Jonathan looked curious, like he had no idea why he was being called to the carpet. Rodney shut the door.

Rebecca gestured for them both to take seats at her desk. "Thanks for coming in. I've called this meeting because there seems to be a conflict of interest that we need to discuss. Jonathan, you are a valuable member of the team, and I see your contributions as being key in getting Branches where it is today. However, your work lately has been haphazard, as well as often late, frequently full of bugs, and not showing the problem-solving flare that we have come to depend on. In addition, it appears that you're moonlighting for another company."

Jonathan looked to have been about to say something in his defense, but his mouth shut when she mentioned "moonlighting." He glanced quickly at Rodney, who was stone-faced and then seemingly found something fascinating about the desk and proceeded to examine it in detail.

Rebecca let the silence stretch.

"I thought I was getting a raise," Jonathan mumbled. "Today?" He then seemed to think through his answer. He sat up straighter. "No, I can see that my performance lately wouldn't merit a raise. But I took the extra work because I need more money, and I wasn't getting a raise here."

So, it's my fault that you didn't talk to me and instead chose to break your contract? The thought was quickly followed by a more disturbing one: *does the team feel they can't talk to me?* Rebecca's gut reaction wasn't a good one, and she knew it. She held her tongue.

Rodney shifted in the silence; he was obviously uncomfortable but mercifully knew better than to break the silence.

Unfortunately, Jonathan had folded his arms and wasn't going to volunteer anything else.

"Your performance, up to a couple of months ago, was rather remarkable. What made you think a raise was not possible?"

"Not, *not* possible. Just not coming soon. I know things are tight around here. I've seen all the signs. But I had some expenses come up, and I needed to bring in more. That's all."

Rebecca was deeply curious as to what "all the signs" were but knew that line of questioning wasn't going to help resolve the real issue at hand here. She chose the more pertinent question. "I usually don't pry into my employees' personal lives, but in this case, I feel I have to. What changed in your financial situation to make your pay here unsatisfactory?"

Jonathan shifted in his chair. He glanced up and made brief eye contact, then returned his gaze to the table. "Leah, she's having complications with the pregnancy. This is our third, and at first, I had to fly her mom down to help take care of the kids. And when the doctor put her on bed rest, it became obvious that we'd need a more long-term solution. My mother-in-law is very nice in small doses. But the kids were too active for her … it just wasn't working out. And nannies are, well, expensive." Jonathan jutted his chin out a bit.

Rebecca's heart hurt for him. "I'm sorry that you're going through this struggle. But it seems like there were some options that you didn't explore before you decided to moonlight."

"Well, I tried to refinance. But that was going to take months, and I needed cash right then. I don't really feel like I did wrong by taking care of my family."

"Did you think to talk to Rodney or myself about the situation?"

"So, you could say 'too bad, so sad.' No thank you. I've been there, done that."

Rebecca sat back a bit in her chair. "I guess we've not done a good job sharing how much we value our team, or maybe you've had a bad experience at a previous employer and assumed that Branches was the same."

"What could you possibly do to help?"

"I'm not sure, but I know we'd have worked with you to find a solution. Off the top of my head, we could have given you more work here, flexibility to work from home, or different hours. But we didn't get the chance to even have that conversation."

Jonathan blinked.

"I think you know I'm a fair person, and I always ask you guys to tell me whenever things are not right, or someone screwed up. I hate surprises because they usually leave me backed into a corner, which is where I'm right now." She sighed heavily. "Jonathan, you're in breach of your employment contract. You need to quit that other job immediately."

"Can I have more work here?"

"Yes, but before you do, I need you to catch your current task load up and fix the bugs in that last round."

"Deal."

"Okay. This weekend is going to be a long one, and I'll be here throughout. I'll expect to see you in."

"Thank you." He was quiet for a moment. "Also, thank you. I know you don't need to do this, and I broke trust. It'll be a lot better just working for you, I promise."

Rebecca nodded, but as the two men left the office, she wondered if she was making the right decision. *Should I have just let him go?*

Bao was a machine. As far as Rebecca could tell, she lived on oolong tea and extra spicy Cheetos. If she had a steady supply, Bao wouldn't look around her screen for hours at a time. It was amazing and frightening to try and have a conversation with someone who wouldn't look your way … and when they finally did, their fingers kept flying over the keyboard on their own.

It was a stark contrast to Jonathan, tip-tapping his way through his code. He was really having trouble settling down and was actually being somewhat disruptive to the programmers that were in the zone.

Rebecca realized that she needed to keep her door open more often to spot these kinds of things. Working all weekend while Richard and Tori were in Miami was a great opportunity to knock some things out on her to-do list and reconnect with the team.

If anyone deserved a raise, she mused, it was Bao. Her English skills had improved greatly over the last few months, and Rebecca noticed that every single desk in the vicinity of Bao's had a battered copy of a Chinese-English dictionary on it. Rebecca loved that her team had come together to embrace Bao. And in return, Bao lifted them with her solid contributions to the code.

So basically, everyone needed a raise. She was going to have to figure out how to make that happen in a few months. Otherwise, her Jonathan problem would spread.

It surprised her to see Rodney churning through contract work. They still needed to take on third-party coding projects to balance the books. What was surprising was that Rodney was having to work weekends to get it done. In the beginning, it was contract work first, Branches second. At some point it had switched, and Rebecca felt like she should be keeping a closer eye on that. What was the percentage of hours her team were working on it now?

In reality, the board didn't want her to take on any more contract work at all. They wanted the company to focus all their energy on the success of Branches. And frankly, it would require a lot more investment on their part, or a lot more user adoption to make the money work. Their desire to focus solely on Branches had come up in the early board of directors' meetings, and Rebecca had only committed to seeing what she could do. Nobody had brought it up in the intervening months, and she had only referred to it on the profit and loss reports as "miscellaneous income" since then.

It was an uneasy situation, and she promised herself (again) to review the books again.

A commotion at the front door distracted her from her thoughts. A gaggle of giggling college-age women were piling into the office. It took her a moment to realize that these must be Laura's sorority sisters here to product test Branches. Sure enough, Laura appeared and started corralling them into desks. She had prepared a tutorial slide show for them, and had Rebecca sign off earlier in the week. Rebecca tipped Laura an encouraging wink and then stepped into her office so Laura wouldn't feel she was looking over her shoulder.

A few hours later, a buzz from her from cellphone broke into the fugue state of the zone. She blinked in surprise. Her to-do list had gotten a lot shorter. But she was also startled to realize it was dark, and the office beyond her door seemed deserted. How long had she been here?

The phone insisted on her attention again.

It was Richard.

"Hey, babe," she said in greeting.

"Hey."

The hair on her arms stood at attention. Rebecca couldn't immediately put her finger on why, but something in his greeting had had her sitting upright and listening intently. "What happened?" Rebecca tried to keep her voice even.

Richard took a noisy, shaky breath on the other end of the line. "I've messed up."

Several very frightening scenarios started populating her brain. He was obviously drunk and upset. Later, she wondered how she could know these things so quickly and have no good reason.

"What did you do?"

"I lost."

"Lost? Lost Tori? Where is Tori?" Rebecca's heart had clutched hard, like she had missed a step on a treacherous staircase.

"Tori's fine. I don't think she knows anything is up yet."

Rebecca squeezed some air into her lungs, trying to get herself to calm down.

And then he said his worst: "No, I lost the money."

"What money."

"We took a cruise over to Bimini. There was stuff for Tori to do on the island, and the casinos are known for their high roller perks."

Rebecca realized her skin was cold and damp.

"I had changed a lot more chips than usual, so I could get the perks. I wasn't planning on gambling it. It was just to get treated like a high roller. I just missed that high-rolling lifestyle. I need to feel seen again. Taken seriously."

A pleading note had entered his voice and it absolutely killed her.

"How much did you lose?"

"The house fund."

"You lost three months of mortgage payments? Our last piece of security if this whole company fails. You gambled it away?"

"I'm sorry."

Rebecca wanted to scream. She wanted to tell Richard what an idiot he was. She wanted to eviscerate him for throwing away her last shred of stability.

But none of that was going to get the money back.

"Richard." She was surprised by how even her voice was. "Sober up. Drink a gallon of water, find our daughter, and put a smile on your face. Make it a memorable and happy few days for her. And when you get back, we're going to look at the accounts and figure out ..." *What? How much we have? How much we needed? Whether I can trust him with anything ever again?* "We'll figure out everything."

When the phone disconnected, she sat at her desk for a long time.

Chapter Fifteen

LAURA CHEERFULLY LEFT THE OFFICE with an approved investors report to send out to the board of directors. The meeting was coming up soon, and Laura was taking point on arranging it again. Rebecca wondered idly if Laura had read and understood those reports. If she knew that the money was coming into and out of the account so fast, it could create a sonic boom. As far as Rebecca could tell, Laura hadn't breathed a word about the financial situation to anyone within the company walls, so maybe she hadn't read them at all.

Her personal funds were depleted, that was the headline news out of the drunken call with Richard. He had broken his own "gamble with bonuses only" rule and dipped into everything. Did he have a gambling problem? She wasn't ready to know. The fight when he got home had been ugly. He tried to make her feel like the gambling was her fault. That she was never around anymore, and always stressed when she was. It was so asinine that she had just left. Just walked out and slept in her office, after diligently changing the passwords on all the banking accounts. He still had his money, but any account that had her money in it now had brand new security features.

Were they over? She felt ill just thinking about it. And the ultimate verdict was another thing she wasn't sure she wanted to know. But right now, it was easier to work, to try to fix her broken company, and deal with her personal life later.

She wouldn't be able to feed the company any personal money. She knew that the day was coming when she would reach the end of her personal resources, but the timeline had always been in the future, staved off by every new client and investor she got. Now she had to face facts. If things didn't turn around, the company would fail.

Lindsey picked up on the first ring.

Several months ago, her former boss had started asking questions a potential investor would. Rebecca had offered to send her an investor packet, and she had enthusiastically agreed to look it over.

"Oh, it's about the investment?" Lindsey asked after a few minutes of chitchat. "Thank goodness. I was worried you were about to tell me that you were behind on the contract work again."

Rebecca fought to reply mildly. "Really? I wasn't aware we had been late at all recently." She knew for a fact that they hadn't missed a deadline in months. Ever since Lindsey had first expressed an interest in investing in Branches, she had made a point of checking the deliveries were on time.

"Well, I guess it has been a while, but it was really inconvenient when it happened, and so now when I think of you, I think of that. Plus, your work always has bugs."

What? Rebecca could see where this was going and didn't like it one bit. She put on her most diplomatic voice. "Hm. Can you give me more details on that? I've been personally looking at the bug list being reported back to us. We are well under the 1.5 percent standard. Is your team returning all bug reports to us or troubleshooting locally?"

"I don't know. I just heard it was buggy."

Rebecca knew for a fact that Lindsey had a spreadsheet in front of her that had every single statistic and number possible for a person to have to quantify someone's work. There was no way she didn't have a bug report in front of her right now.

"Okay, well please check with your team. If there's a problem and they aren't alerting us, then we don't have an opportunity to improve. You know that I pride myself on the details."

"I guess. Thanks, I'll have my team look."

A few minutes later, Rebecca ended the call. There was no point in discussing the investment. Lindsey was throwing around unfounded quality issues as a way to put off having the conversation. There was no way she was going to invest, at least not right now.

Rebecca was tempted to just cancel Lindsey's contract work altogether. The board didn't want her to take contract work anymore. If she could land just two more investors, maybe she could wrap it all up and kick it to the curb.

But in her heart, she knew Lindsey's objections had nothing to do with contract work and everything to do with Branches' financial statements. Rebecca put it in her notes to double-check the quality control and call Lindsey next month. Hopefully, Lindsey would be willing to at least talk through the investment then.

In the meantime, she had a list of people to call to see if she could land some much-needed money. But first, she needed a friendly pep talk.

> **Lindsey is bailing on the investment. Heard anything on the grapevine?**

TRAVIS—AIRPORT SQUAD: *Oh Geez. I should have texted you so you wouldn't waste your time! It is so bad over there. She has zero credibility left.*

> **You're kidding! What did she do?**

A GIF materialized of someone spectacularly face-planting off playground equipment.

TRAVIS—AIRPORT SQUAD: *Rumor has it that she blustered her way into the role and then hasn't delivered on a single thing she promised. She just sits behind her spreadsheets and isn't leading any of the initiatives that they hired her for.*

> **Paralysis by analysis?**

TRAVIS—AIRPORT SQUAD: *Maybe. But it sounded like all she wants to do is maintain everything exactly as it is.*

Rebecca thought back to her time working for Lindsey. Had she ever led a new initiative? Or had it always fallen to Rebecca and Valarie to manage?

> **Heard anything about Valarie recently?**

TRAVIS—AIRPORT SQUAD: *Nope. Why?*

> **Eh. Just trying to add to my "potential investor pool."**

TRAVIS—AIRPORT SQUAD: *Did you ever connect with that guy from the Vegas conference?*

Which guy?

TRAVIS—AIRPORT SQUAD: *LOL. The guy that keeps calling you.*

I miss fifty calls a day, mostly scammers trying to get me to make payments on a student loan I paid off a decade ago.

TRAVIS—AIRPORT SQUAD: *Well, the next time he calls, try to answer.*

Send me his number, I'll put him under First Name: Vegas, Last Name: Dude. I'm assuming you don't remember his name or company.

TRAVIS—AIRPORT SQUAD: *First name is Calvin. That's all I got on the voicemail he left me, nudging me to nudge you.*

Alright, consider me nudged. Send the number my way and I'll try to pick it up.

———

"Boss? We need to talk." Rodney's knuckles were still rapping on the doorframe as he let himself in and hastily shut the door behind him.

Rebecca braced herself for the worst. "What is it?"

"Remember all those cute sorority girls who came in here a couple weekends ago?"

"Yes?"

"They've completely fucked us."

Rebecca's head rocked back with surprise. Rodney never cursed. "What happened?"

"They were idiots. Absolute morons. They didn't understand what they were doing at all. The testing feedback and instructions completely corrupted the process. It's nonsense, completely circular logic. And our Indian programmers have been following that circle of crazy for weeks."

Rebecca could feel the blood draining from her face. "No one checked it before it was sent?"

"Laura was supposed to. Either she didn't do any quality control, or Laura has no idea what it is we do here."

"Oh no. I approved the training materials." Rebecca would have to pull them back out to see where the disconnect happened. But that wasn't the priority here.

"How bad is it."

"Well, as near as I can tell, we've been chasing our own tails for weeks. And I have no idea how many problems have been introduced into the code in that time. I think we have to delay the latest release and revert back to code before the testing round ever started."

"Do we even still have the clean code?"

There was a knock at the door; they both ignored it.

Rodney gave her a smug look. "Version control is the core tenet of my faith in the Almighty. It has saved me on multiple occasions."

"So, we revert, bring in a new round of testers, and what? What am I not seeing here?"

"Late release, more expense, lost time."

The knock came again, a little more insistently.

"Okay, revert, let's go for the professional testers this time too."

"Hallelujah."

"Come in!" Rebecca raised her voice to the door.

Jonathan's head peeked in around the door. "I'm really glad to catch you both together," he said nervously. "Uh." He looked down at a creased envelope in his hands. "I want to thank you for the opportunity to work with you. But I quit." Jonathan looked as if he would hand the letter of resignation to Rodney but thought better of it and deposited the letter on Rebecca's desk instead.

Rebecca eyed the letter warily. "Am I correct to guess that the other company you were working for made you an offer you couldn't refuse?"

"No. This is a different company. But yes, there is a pay bump, and I know you can't match, so I'm not going to make you try."

Rebecca considered and then shrugged. "If that's how you feel, I wish you the best. Is this effective immediately?"

Jonathan nodded.

Rodney shifted like he was going to say something, but then he settled.

"Alright, I'll draw up your final pay. Do you mind telling us who you're going to?"

Jonathan smiled tightly. "Octopus."

Rebecca forced a smile in return while she internally raged. *Oh, Octopus pays so much, do they? We couldn't possibly match it?*

She shut the door after Rodney and Jonathan. Rodney had tipped her a knowing look, and she was certain that Jonathan was about to walk out the door with an escort at his heels.

Well, Octopus is welcome to have my worst programmer and overpay him. Best of luck to them both — may they choke on it. And how did the magnificent Laura screw up so badly? Or did I screw up by jumping at the chance for cheap, zero experience testing of a complicated product?

The answer, of course, was an unequivocal "Yes, I did!"

But it was the bigger question, what to do about it, that caused her to pause.

It was all too much, all of it. And what could she possibly do about any of it?

————

The board meeting was going better than expected. The usual players were there – Travis, Don, Louise, Arun, and Michael. Albert, who had met the board and made the investment, was there to observe, as well as Liz.

Even with the extra people in attendance, things were clicking along. Sixty minutes into the 90-minute agenda, Rebecca's asks were getting very little pushback. The board had agreed that due to expense and convenience issues, the next few months would be virtual meetings. This would take the burden of hosting off of Branches, and she would just have to provide a video link versus an entire spread of food, drinks, and renting the room.

Rebecca had been nervous to say that the latest release was three weeks behind. She had prepared an explanation that didn't include sorority girls and botched quality control, as well as weeks of chasing their tale. She had stayed up numerous nights kicking herself about that debacle and the possible fall out. She had even over-prepared a meeting with Laura to discuss the disconnect between the training materials and the outcome of the testing, how it had happened, where the oversight had been needed, and try as she might, Laura had cried. Then Rebecca cried, and they both picked themselves back up and moved forward to fix it.

And now, after all the stress, scrambling, and frantic planning ... nothing. The board gave a collective shrug, a few questions and ... that was it. Rebecca wasn't sure what to do with that pit of anxiety now that it was no longer necessary to hold onto it.

When reviewing the sales metrics, everyone seemed impressed that the average sales cycle was shortening. The current issue was that the lead quality had predictably dropped, as Rebecca's rolodex got thinner. This would mean the sales cycle would increase again if they didn't take proactive steps. She saw her board come together to spitball the issue of getting quality leads into the pipeline and actively contribute to the solution.

Now, to the sticky part of the meeting: expenses.

"Spending last month was twenty percent over budget. There were a few things that contributed to the overspend. We had to make a reinvestment in the company. We needed to buy a few more servers and license the software we needed for the expansion. There was a marketing opportunity at an upcoming conference, and we needed to pay upfront to secure it. Additionally, we had an unexpected bill from the state. Apparently, there was a problem with our workers compensation insurance, and they fined us for the discrepancy."

"All of these are reasonable, and I can see how they happened," Michael began. "But it seems like these are the kinds of things that will come up continually as Branches grows, and so they should be part of the budget."

"Our projected monthly overhead does balance with our current income," Rebecca countered, trying not to be defensive. "This was just a month where a bunch of one-off expenses came due."

"I understand," Michael said. "But if you have a home budget that you're always blowing because a tire needs repair, or the tax bill is coming due, you have to work it into the overall budget. Otherwise, the budget is meaningless."

"I'm actually more concerned with the income," Arun jumped in.

Rebecca felt her eyebrows clench with confusion. "The income?"

"Yes, the income doesn't add up. I've been watching this miscellaneous income for months. What is this miscellaneous income? Why is it there?"

Crap.

Rebecca tried to pick her words carefully. "Miscellaneous is any income coming into the company that was not generated by the Branches product. There were a few income streams that I used as I was building and financing the business. Some of the marketing videos I put on YouTube are monetized and bring in sporadic income. We fiddled around with some affiliate links as well that occasionally spit out money. And we took on contract work in the beginning, and that is being phased out as well."

"What kind of contract work?"

"When I started the company, I didn't have investors, so I was able to build the company by having eighty percent of hours spent in contract work to corporations while twenty percent of the hours was spent on Branches. After the beta launch, we started phasing out contract work and adjusting the mix of Branches hours versus contract hours. At this point, it's about flipped with eighty percent Branches, twenty percent contract work."

"This is unacceptable!" Arun said. He looked around the room, clearly searching for support.

Everyone looked distinctly uncomfortable, looking anywhere but her or Arun.

Michael cleared his throat. "I have to agree, Rebecca. This arrangement … the investors … we understand that contract work was a necessity when you started it. But we invested in Branches, not a contract coding house. Not only does that mean the priorities of the company are divided, but the income of Branches has been overstated since the beginning. I don't think I would have invested if this had been disclosed."

Rebecca's jaw was on the floor. A thousand thoughts were swirling in her head. "It was on the paperwork the entire time," she said faintly. "I haven't hidden anything."

"Well, it certainly wasn't clear that twenty percent of the income was coming from contract work, and not a viable Branches product. Plus, you're twenty percent over budget. That's a hell of a gap."

"I can't stop the contract work until we have more income. The books don't work at all."

"I think we need to call an executive session," Michael said.

Rebecca looked at him sharply, "What does that mean?"

"It means you and Don need to leave the room, and we're going to talk about you."

Don moved to pick up his papers.

Rebecca looked around the room, frozen. Liz met her eyes and gave her a sympathetic nod. Rebecca blinked. This was really happening.

A few blurry moments later, she was out in the hall.

Don came out of the room, his lips pressed tightly together, obviously trying to hold something in.

"What can they do?" Rebecca blurted.

"A lot of things, there's—" Don started.

Liz entered the hallway, followed closely by Albert. Liz looked uncomfortable and Albert was … angry?

He certainly amped up. "Why didn't you give me a seat on the board?"

"Um. What?" Rebecca questioned.

"Executive session is only for sitting board members, so I have to sit in the hallway while they figure out what to do about my investment."

"I'm not happy about being out here either," Rebecca retorted.

"I told you that a board's job is to make you accountable. Make sure you weren't taking money from the company payroll. But this is so much worse, Rebecca. They could take your job for this."

"They couldn't." Rebecca gasped. A quick glance at Liz and Don confirmed that it very well could happen.

"Over my cold, dead body."

Albert made an indistinct, but skeptical, noise at the back of his throat.

"Does this make you happy, Albert, coming here to say I told you so? Well, let me tell you, I have put ten times what you invested into my own company and nine months of sweat equity on top of that. I have a lot more to lose here than you, and I will not lose."

Albert opened his mouth to retort, but Liz got in there first, breaking in loudly, "Albert, I hear there's a lovely garden on top of this building with a wine bar. They're going to be a while yet. How about you let me buy you a glass? It'll be nice to have some fresh air while we wait. They'll call us when it is time to come back, won't you, Rebecca?"

Rebecca nodded, grateful that Liz was getting Albert out of firing range. A few moments later the hallway was just her and Don propping up the walls. The thick door was muffling a heated conversation that was always just out of reach of hearing. Mostly she could just hear her own panicked breathing.

"Could I really lose the company?" she asked Don.

"Yes," Don said, "but it seems unlikely in this case."

"Why?"

"They invested in you, not Branches, not really. Branches was barely viable when you went looking for investors. So, they didn't place their bet on Branches, they placed it on your personality, skills, experience, and frankly, your absolute determination of will. They wanted their money to be doubled by you. Now they see that you'll do what it takes to make the company work. It shook them, because it feels like broken trust, but they aren't going to fire you."

"You sound like you've seen this before."

Don shrugged. "Occasionally, but the only CEO I've seen removed deserved it."

"What did they do?"

"Among other things, he did a bunch of cocaine right before walking into the board meeting."

"I bet that killed a bunch of trust."

"Yep. No one could defend him after that."

"The bar for firing a woman has to be lower though. The patriarchy can't handle a flawed woman."

"Don't go borrowing that trouble. The bottom line is that none of them really know the product, and there is no natural new leader at hand to plug into the CEO seat. Unless Travis is in there making a case to replace you, I think you'll be alright."

What? Travis would never. Would he?

Rebecca and Don said very little after that.

———

Thirty minutes later, the door opened. Travis and Michael stepped out. Travis looked pale.

Michael was the first to speak. "We've been sent out to talk with each of you individually. Don, you got me."

"And I got you." Travis smiled awkwardly. "Want to go to your office?"

Rebecca nodded.

They said nothing in the elevator or in the hallway as they walked back to the Branches office. Rebecca had no idea how to start, and it seemed that Travis didn't either.

It was only when they were safe behind her office door that she dared to ask, "Are they firing me?"

"No."

Rebecca sat down, boneless at her desk. She scrubbed her temples with both hands, trying to make the news sink in quicker.

"I wasn't sure since we had to talk in private. Christ, that was like walking to the gallows."

"Oh, shit. I'm sorry. There are things we have to discuss, but I didn't want to start in public." He looked genuinely sorry, and Rebecca smiled at him, feeling suddenly very generous.

"Okay, lay it on me. What's the message?"

"Well, the feeling from the board is that you deliberately mislead them. They want to make sure that you understand the problem that broken trust presents."

"I should have been more forthcoming, I know that. I feel terrible about it."

"They want you to terminate all the remaining contract work. How many contracts are left?"

"Just one. For Lindsey. I should have cut it off a long time ago, it has been scope creeping for a while. She's a total pain, but the checks come on time, and they're paying premium rates. And I thought if I continued to deliver on time, that she'd invest. And I need that money," she took a deep breath. "Travis, absolutely everything I have is in this company."

"I know."

Rebecca fought hard to keep the tears from spilling over. "I mean *everything.*"

Travis looked her in the eyes. "I know."

She nodded, pursing her lips, worried that as soon as she took a breath she'd start really crying. She didn't have time to do that, she needed to get through this moment and then deal with her feelings afterwards.

"You're going to have to cancel that contract. I think we both know that Lindsey isn't going to invest. She's not going to take that kind of risk. But there will be other investors who will. We just need to get through this speed bump and then we'll be back on track."

"Does the board have a solution for the income shortfall?" Rebecca asked.

"A lot of options are on the table. Raising prices, cutting heads, adding premium levels, more introductions to buyers and investors. They're coming together on that part right now while you and I are in here. But nothing will be decided until you get back in there and let them know you are sorry and that you've canceled the contracts."

"I can do that."

"Okay, but there's one other thing you need to know …"

The board reconvened twenty minutes later, with everyone present, including Liz and Albert.

Rebecca's stomach was clenched uncomfortably, and her arms felt jittery, like she had just lifted an impossible weight. Like she wouldn't be able to lift anything ever again.

Even though Travis had let her know what to expect, Rebecca still eyed the group warily. If they had changed their minds while Travis was speaking with her, she didn't want to be blindsided.

That said, no one at the table looked happy. But that might be a good sign for her. No one looked like they had succeeded at pushing through their own agenda in their absence.

She took a breath, then took the bull by the horns. "Before we proceed, I do want to apologize. It wasn't my intention to misrepresent any of the financials, and I can completely understand why you were upset. The categorization system was a mistake, but it was not intended to hide anything."

"I, uh appreciate that," Michael said. "Did Travis explain the accountability plan to you?"

Rebecca was trying desperately to swallow her pride and not choke on it. She had too much invested in the company to quit. And the humiliation of getting called to the carpet like this was threatening to burn her up. She was not going to cry, she refused to cry, she was not going to cry. "Yes," she replied, her voice wavering. She took a steadying breath. "But I haven't had a chance to discuss it with Don yet." She looked over at Don.

Michael asked, "Don, do you know what has been proposed?"

"Yes, and if Rebecca is okay with it, I can make it work."

"Okay, so let's go ahead and lay it out here in the room so there are no misunderstandings. Rebecca, for the immediate future, Don is going to be in control of the purse strings. He's going to pay the bills, authorize any transactions outside of the normal expenditures, and create the reports. There will be no categorizations of income, or any other slight-of-hand to make things look rosier than they are. We want complete transparency as to what is going on. Don, do you think you can handle that?"

"Yes."

Michael was being diplomatic, and kind. But Arun had his arms folded, looking like he would spit nails. Rebecca deeply regretted ever allowing him to invest.

"Rebecca," Michael continued, "we're going to give this a try for a few months and see how we all feel. Frankly, you're doing too many jobs right now. And the job that is the most critical to the success of Branches is sales. You're invaluable as the face of the company, and a lot of the early success was due to leveraging your relationships. By taking the day-to-day financial burden off your plate, we want to free up your time and mental bandwidth to go out and grow the customer base. And in a few months, if things are on the right track, we'll revisit Don's role and day-to-day responsibilities. But my hope is that this works for both of you, and that Rebecca, you are so successful in bringing new clients in, that you have no need to take the financials back on a daily basis."

"I can live with that." Rebecca wished she had something better to say, but she absolutely refused to say anything that might sound like gratitude. She didn't have it in her to be gracious about this.

Michael looked around the table. "Does anyone else having anything to add?"

Arun shifted but remained silent. Liz caught her eye and nodded. Albert was clearly studying Don but didn't seem to have anything to add.

"Okay, then I believe this meeting is adjourn—"

A sharp knock rapped on the conference room door.

Rebecca gave a shrug to Michael. "I guess the next meeting is ready for their room."

A head popped in. It was Laura.

"I'm so sorry, Rebecca, can I borrow you for a moment?" Laura's lips were pinched tight – completely unlike her usual self.

"Sure, we just wrapped." Rebecca glanced at the board members. "Excuse me."

Laura was actually wringing her hands in the hall. She hastily shut the door behind Rebecca so no one inside could hear. She pushed Rebecca's cell phone into her hand. "Your husband's been calling every five minutes. Your daughter is missing."

Chapter Sixteen

HOW IN THE HOLY MOTHER *of all that is good on this Earth have I ended up here?* It was one of the many thoughts cycling quickly through her head. Along with: *where is Tori; you almost lost control of your own company, you idiot; is Tori safe; am I completely wrong about everything in my life; and Tori, pick up your damn phone.*

Rebecca was spinning her wheels, literally. She couldn't stand waiting at home, so she was driving around every teenager-ish hangout she could think of: the high school, the tennis courts, and the movie theater (where the manager on duty had eyed her warily but agreed to keep an eye out). Now she was randomly driving the streets of downtown, navigating traffic and paying more attention to the pedestrians than the road.

Richard was at home dialing everyone Tori knew, trying to remotely turn on her geolocation and obviously racking his brain for any other solution that might assist in tracking down his daughter.

Tori had gone to school, it seemed. The friends Richard had managed to talk to confirmed they had seen her in class. There had been no "absent" notices sent to her or Richard, and the school portal showed work turned in today. But sometime after 3 P.M., she had evaporated. Didn't take the bus, and her best buddy that sometimes gave her a ride wasn't even in the state this week. Her parents had taken her out of school for an enrichment trip to New York. And Rebecca just knew that had to eat at Tori. Her best friend was watching Broadway plays and wandering through the Met. And all she got was a booze cruise to a rundown casino where her father gambled away the house money and then got drunk and cried.

Rebecca stuffed down the blame. Obviously, things had gone wrong. For Tori, for her marriage, for her company. But there was a way out. She knew there had to be. She just needed a moment to think.

And to find her daughter.

A bright flash of light from a street corner startled Rebecca. *Oh, damn it!* She had run a red light, just coasted on through it like it wasn't there. And the auto ticket camera had snapped her picture. There would be a $200 ticket in the mail next week that she didn't know how she would pay.

She swerved into the first available parking spot and beat on her steering wheel until her hands ached and she was slightly calmer.

Be smart about this, she scolded herself.

For a moment, she held her phone, thinking. No bus, no friend to give Tori a ride. Sure, other people had cars, but … Rebecca opened her credit card app. There it was. A pending charge for Chariot, the local rideshare app.

Okay, so she had connected Tori's rideshare app to her credit card almost two years ago. Tori would have been fourteen. There was no way she wouldn't have set up a way to track where her daughter went to. She checked her email for the receipt, but it wasn't there.

Is it so recent that there isn't a receipt yet? Had she unsubscribed or blocked Chariot in some way? A quick check of her junk folder revealed she had no emails from them, ever. But she knew she had received them at some point.

A red Tesla.

Why was she remembering that Tesla? When had she ... *OH!*

Her brain had made the connection for her. Her Chariot account was connected to her old corporate email address. She had deleted the app when she had quit. Okay, so one mystery solved.

It took a few minutes to recover her account and enter her new email address.

And the recent trip was to ... the country club? They hadn't had a membership there in months, but maybe Tori connected with a friend. Was there a teen social tonight? On a weekday night? Not likely. But where else could she go from there?

Rebecca didn't stop to think, just drove. Even if Tori wasn't there currently, someone there would know something. She just had to get there.

———

Twenty minutes later, she zoomed up to the gatehouse. The guard recognized her and waived her through. It was the first good break she'd had all day and was immensely grateful that she wouldn't have to explain about her missing daughter and beg to get in. She hadn't thought she could manage it and keep from crying at the same time.

Rebecca parked sloppily, not caring. She had no idea where Tori was but figured if there was some kind of event going on, it would be at the main building. She was disappointed that the entrance was quiet. The events board was in its normal position and Rebecca hustled over to it.

Nothing there seemed remotely likely to attract a teenager. Maybe she was having dinner with a friend's family?

Rebecca was so busy looking for her daughter at a table that she almost didn't spot her behind the hostess station. "What are you doing?" The words were out of her mouth without thinking.

It was obvious what her daughter was doing. She was working.

Tori looked startled out at her from a face full of carefully applied make-up. She was wearing all black, sensible heels, and could easily pass as a college student.

Fear, relief, anger, confusion, they were all scrabbling to grab the wheel. Rebecca tried to take a breath, get some control.

"I—" Tori started and then looked away. She looked like she was fighting back tears.

"Why didn't you tell me you got a job?" Rebecca was proud that her voice was even, not accusing.

"I don't know."

"Tori. You can tell me. It's okay."

"I want to go to prom and know there isn't any—" Tori bit her lip, obviously picking her words carefully. "I know things are tight. And I didn't want to—"

Ah crap. I'm a shitty parent. I can't provide for my kid, and she knows it. "You didn't want to ask for money because you were afraid we didn't have it."

Tori nodded at a place on the floor. "And I didn't want you to fight again."

Ugh! And she's trying to protect our marriage too "So, you got a hostessing job?"

Tori nodded at the floor again.

Shit shit shit. I can't yell at her. Not for this. "Okay, I need you to look at me right now. In the eyes." Rebecca struggled to smile, to infuse some warmth, some love, into her voice.

Tori reluctantly met her eyes. "Don't be mad."

"I have a lot of feelings right now. I'm mad you didn't tell me. But mostly I'm just so very proud of you. You wanted to change things for yourself, and you went out and did something about it. There's nothing to be ashamed about working."

A tear slipped out of Tori's eye, and Rebecca hurried to brush it away. "It's okay, don't cry. It'll take forever to reapply that make-up if you cry it off." She hugged Tori and felt Tori take a deep breath and let it out slowly. Tori gave her a tighter squeeze and Rebecca let her go.

"What time are you done working?"

"Ten."

"That's really late for a weeknight. Did you really think we wouldn't miss you?"

Tori shrugged.

"I'll wait out in the parking lot for you. Come out when you're done, okay? I'll drive you home."

Tori hugged her again. "Thanks, Mom."

———

Rebecca wandered the dark grounds of the country club. The golf range was lit and a few members swinging. She didn't go that way, preferring to slink around in the gloom. She wandered past the deserted 19th hole. She had never been a great golfer but had enjoyed the sunshine and the time with Richard between the tees. It broke her heart that she might never do that again.

Her relationship with Richard was more strained now than any other time in their marriage. Not even those first few months of being parents were as detrimental to their marriage as starting a business had been. And how dare he go gambling and then blame her for it? Her board of directors lost faith in her for misclassifying some money. He had done far worse. How would they ever come back from that?

Her feet carried her down the path from the golf course. The tennis courts were dark. She wistfully peeked at them from a distance, mindful not to set off the motion sensor lights. Years ago, she used to play with Tori here. It was something they would look forward to doing together every week. And then, it had stopped. She couldn't remember when, or why. But one day, Tori was playing with her, and the next she was playing with a coach and a team. Living an independent life.

It stung that Tori was working to make her own money. She had created this company to provide a better life for her daughter. Not make her so stressed out about money that she took on her own job rather than to ask for a dress. What a complete failure of a mom she had turned out to be.

And yeah, yeah. She raised an independent, strong daughter who decided to take matters into her own hands and take action. Good for her. But also, she hadn't thought it through, went to work on her mother's credit card, and was the lowest paid entry-level position in the building. The dishwasher was likely getting paid more. And what about her grades? If she was working to all hours, how would she ever get into a good college? Did Tori think she wouldn't be able to go to college because her parents couldn't afford it?

Could they still afford it?

If Rebecca lost the company, they definitely couldn't.

The realization hit her like a ton of bricks. She let herself into the pool area and sat pensively on the diving board. The yellow pool lights didn't quite illuminate the distant bottom. Rebecca considered swimming down there, fully clothed, and maybe never resurfacing. That would simplify things, wouldn't it?

She gave herself a mental shake. That was a very permanent solution to a temporary problem. She could never do that to Tori.

But things couldn't keep going the way they were. That way led to failure, bankruptcy, and divorce.

Did she want a divorce?

Getting nose to nose with herself, she could see clearly that the answer was 'no.' But she needed Richard to be someone she could trust, and right now that was broken, and she didn't know how to repair it. She hadn't broken it, and he had to want to fix it too. And her heart ached badly because she didn't know if he wanted to fix their marriage.

Oh shit.

She dialed Richard.

He answered on the first ring. "Did you find her?"

"Yes, she's okay. We'll be home in a couple hours."

"A couple hours? Where are you?"

"Well, you might want to sit down for this. We're at the country club. And we're going to be home in a couple hours because that's when Tori's shift at the restaurant ends."

A few minutes later, Rebecca had explained about the rideshare, and finding Tori working as a hostess at the country club.

"But why? Why did she get a job?" Richard sounded genuinely confused.

"Well, this is the part I'm having feelings about. She knows that money is tight around the house right now. She's felt the belt tightening and apparently heard around enough corners to conclude that we are broke. Too broke to buy her a prom dress."

Richard swore. "That's ridiculous!"

"And so being a young independent woman, she went out and got herself a hostessing job."

"We'll buy her a dress."

"I don't think it's about the dress, Richard. I think that she knows we're fighting about money and is afraid asking for more money is going to lead to more fighting." Rebecca hesitated. "Or a divorce."

"We're not getting a divorce, Rebecca."

"We're not ..." She wasn't sure if it came out as a statement or a question.

"No, we're not. We're going to get through this, maybe get some counseling, but we're never giving up on each other."

"Good." A tear slid down her face. "I wasn't sure." Another tear went gliding down to her chin.

"I know I did a shitty thing and then blamed it on you. It wasn't fair."

Rebecca was scared to know the answer, but she had to ask the question. "Do you have a gambling addiction?"

There was a long silence on the phone.

"I don't think so," he said slowly. "That night wasn't about gambling, I don't know how to explain it, but it wasn't about the risk or the reward. It was like when you've been on a strict diet and suddenly you find yourself surrounded by all the things you told yourself you couldn't have. It wasn't a need to gamble, it was a need to have our old life back, where it didn't matter if I splurged or pissed away a bonus." He sighed. "It was really immature."

There was silence as they both got lost in their own thoughts.

"I almost lost the company today," Rebecca confessed and then told him about the board meeting. "I feel like a complete failure. One of my programmers left to go to my competitors, and I'm sure they're all just laughing their heads off. I mismanaged a quality control thing, and it caused all this extra work, and I can just hear them laughing too. And then today, almost losing control of my own business? I feel like I made a huge mistake by starting this company."

"I don't."

Rebecca was surprised by how quickly and confidently he answered.

"I know the company's in a rough spot right now, and you're stressed. But once you had the idea of starting your own company, there was no going back. You were going to be miserable punching a clock and letting other people make the big decisions. You were born to forge your own path."

"I'm not sure."

"Let me ask you this then."

She could hear the smile in his voice.

"Can you ever imagine working for someone else again? Pulling reports for Lindsey, letting her sit at the head of the table?"

"No. I'm at the head of the table even though I prefer to sit on the side."

"Exactly. So, as the CEO of Branches, what is going to be the next step, and how can I help?"

"I think I need to bring in some big money. High-roller money."

"Now you're talking."

Chapter Seventeen

LESS THAN A MONTH LATER, Rebecca sat in the first-class club at Phoenix Sky Harbor Airport. Arrayed on the table in front of her was a smorgasbord of business cards. The Venture Capital conference in Scottsdale had been successful-ish. It had been exactly the room she needed to be in – big names, all who were looking for opportunities to invest.

The frustrating part of the conference, she reflected, had been the way it was structured, around golfing mostly, and prioritizing small gatherings over large groups. It made it hard to get a feel for how big the conference was, how many were investors versus entrepreneurs, and to casually connect with people. It had been a technology VC Conference, so there had been a big opportunity, and because it was spread so widely, she wasn't sure how well she had taken advantage of it.

That said, she still had made an impressive number of connections.

Thus, the business cards laid out by when and where she met each person. Grouping it this way jogged her memory. She jotted down notes of what each person looked like, what their conversation was like, and anything she might need to slip into a follow-up email.

She was so engrossed in the task that she was startled when Travis appeared at table carrying two drinks.

"Oh geez," she clutched her chest. "I totally lost track of time!"

"Sorry, sorry. I bring offerings of whisky and bitters."

"I guess you're forgiven, then." She smiled, peeking over his shoulder curiously. Rebecca had known that Travis had worked out a long layover to meet up with her on his way to a sales meeting, but she thought it would just be the two of them. A vaguely familiar man was with Travis. Her first impression was money. The man wore a crisp blue shirt, black slacks and shoes that probably cost more than all the purses in her closet. And he wore them all like a second skin.

Travis gave her an emphatic look and raised the glass slightly higher than her reach.

She took the hint to stand.

"Rebecca, I'd like to introduce you to Calvin Sharp. He and I connected at the Vegas tradeshow about eight months ago, but I wasn't able to introduce you then."

"Calvin, so nice to meet you. Were you here for the Cactus and Capitalist Conference?"

"I was! And it's so nice to finally meet you. I tried calling you a few months ago, but we weren't able to connect. Don't feel bad. Being busy means you're working, and that's what I like in technology companies, entrepreneurs who are getting stuff done."

"Well, thank you. But I'm sorry if I didn't return your phone call. How was the conference?"

"Oh, these things are about high rollers trying to one up each other, on the golf course and in the board room. It's all just ways to put new notches on our belts. How about you? Was it a successful conference?"

She glanced down at the cards on the table. "To be honest, I'm not sure. It was hard to tell if I picked the winning track or not."

"Which one were you in? I don't remember seeing your name on my schedule."

"Women in Technology." The category had seemed like the no-brainer track to be on. A way to stand out. But no one had jumped up and down immediately and pledged millions of dollars to see Branches succeed. And her rooms had been half-full at best, but maybe all the rooms were only fifty percent attended. It was so hard to tell.

"That explains it," Calvin said brightly. "I was over in the Enterprise Solutions group."

"Oh." She didn't quite know what she should ask next, but he seemed comfortable taking the conversational lead.

"I see you met all the movers and shakers." He gestured to the table. "Do you mind?"

Rebecca shook her head, and he took a seat and entertained himself perusing the cards as she and Travis settled in.

"This guy doesn't have a pot to piss in," he commented and moved a card to the side of the table. He moved another one on top of the first. "And this guy is going to want a controlling interest, and to flex that control at the worst possible times." Two more cards were culled from the pile without reason stated. "I know this guy." He held a bright green business card up for display. "He's a straight shooter." He started a new pile and quickly added a few more names to it. "I'm doing this, just so you know, because I want to start with a foundation of honesty."

Rebecca smiled. "I appreciate honesty. And foundations. It means we're about to build something."

"Maybe. Just maybe …" A few more cards were sorted off the table. "I was impressed with your company when I met Travis here before. Enough that I remembered him at a random first-class lounge half a year later."

Travis raised a glass in appreciation.

"If I remember correctly, you have a corporate solution for job scheduling, is that right?" Calvin asked.

"Yes, you must have an excellent memory."

"And it's adaptable for health care as well as transactional services."

"Right again, we've rolled out to quite a few industries, but we're mostly focused on consumer product high-volume transactional companies at the moment."

Calvin scratched his chin and looked at the ceiling meditatively. "Have you given any thought to being purchased by one of the big boys? Like Oracle or Cisco?"

"Not really," Rebecca said with a shrug. "Always seemed to me that a company like Oracle or Cisco could build something like we're doing from scratch. They have the resources."

"Hm." He made it sound like an indictment. "They could … and the build or buy option is always on the table. But those guys prefer to buy the leading change agent, if possible. They look to spot industry disrupters and acquire them. I can see that as being a fit for your business."

"I'm sorry, Calvin, I don't mean to sound rude. But are you a broker?"

"Talent scout might be a better term. I like to spot new technology, new solutions, and make introductions."

"Travis, that sounds like a job you'd be good at."

Calvin nodded. "He's good at talking, and I think you're good at building. That combination, the two of you could start and spin off a dozen winning companies."

"And you would arrange all the introductions." Rebecca grinned at him.

"I'm the Chief Business Development officer for Huron, so I'm quite good at it." He gave her a wink and waved dismissively at the pile of cards. "But if you want to keep your company and stay in complete control of it, then one of these cards might help you with it."

"Well, you certainly have given me something to think about."

He produced a card and placed it into the center of the cleared table. "My plane is going to board without me. But please give it a think and give me a call."

A few moments later, they had shaken hands, and he had departed for his gate.

Rebecca flopped back down into her lounge chair. She looked incredulously at Travis. "Did that just happen?"

It took all of her willpower not to call Calvin when she got home. She felt anxious, like a teenager, unsure how to begin this courtship. It took some Googling and texting with Travis to decide, and in fact, dating rules did apply and she needed to wait at least three days. On the third day, she called him after lunch, and he returned the message and set up an official call for the following day.

A breathless conversation later, Rebecca was excited and confused. Huron was definitely interested in something. They had invited her out to meet them in person at their offices in California. But it hadn't been clear if the meeting was to discuss an investment or a purchase offer. And she could absolutely kick herself for not asking directly. But they did set a time and date, and they gave her the contact information for an executive assistant to help coordinate the details.

So, she called Don to her office the following day. And wow, Rebecca wished she had filmed Don's reaction. His perpetual frown lines vanished, and a genuine grin emerged as she explained about the airport meeting. It was a fleeting moment, and his forehead quickly morphed back into the topography of worry, but she was happy she had seen it.

"We're going to need to do a lot of prep work," Don said. He looked pleased at the prospect.

"Yep. But I think it will be worth it."

"Me too."

Things had been a little awkward since Don had been tapped to take over financial decisions for the company. He had asked some clarifying questions in the beginning, leaving her with the distinct impression that some of her decisions had been terribly wrong. They had both tried to make it work, and the shift in responsibilities had, in fact, freed up more time to develop the business. But losing total control had chafed. It wasn't until right this moment that Rebecca was very grateful for his support.

This was doubly true since she was running on next to no sleep because her brain had been running all night. *Does Huron want to buy or invest? Do I want to sell or keep going? Would deep pockets solve our problems or create more pressure and oversight? Would selling be abandoning all the people who helped me? Betray the trust of my support squad?* It had gone on like that until dawn, when she finally decided that no matter what, she had a fiduciary responsibility to her investors to explore this opportunity. And like magic, her brain finally showed mercy and allowed her to squeak two hours of sleep in.

If she was going to sell the company, it was going to be a team effort. And if this turned out to be a major investment in Branches, then she would need the team too, if only to structure oversight better than it was now. She was not going to trade money for extra stress – Arun had already taught her that lesson.

Don immediately got down to business. The whiteboard filled as he laid out his questions and concerns in erasable marker. Thirty minutes later, they had roughly five categories of prep work with various questions, reminders and statistics piled underneath each heading.

Product Road Map – Huron would of course want to know everything about what they were developing and the features for each release. This category included a Branches overview, where they were unique in the marketplace, customer feedback and feature requests, and the timeline for development of the next phase.

Customer Pipeline – Rebecca would need to be able to present the who, the whys, the how's of customer acquisition. This would need to include the details of their prospecting process and sales cycle.

Team – Branches was built on a team of talented programmers. They additionally had support people and a slew of positions that would need to be added as the company continued to grow. She would have to be able to show the strength of the current team plus the plan for recruitment and training.

Financial Projections – Admittedly her weak point, but Don was fairly confident he could prep some numbers that would work. Apparently, they would need to pad it liberally, as that was expected, and any numbers submitted would be automatically adjusted downward by thirty percent. That felt uncomfortably close to what she and the board had just punched out, but Don assured her that this was an industry standard in the investment/acquisition world.

Investment Concerns – What amount of money would they need to contribute to make the investment worthwhile? What guardrails could be put in place to keep control of the company and not spend all her time reporting and answering to oversight?

Acquisition Concerns – So many questions here … if they wanted to acquire rather than invest. They included practical things like timeline, price, and process. The more abstract concerns included history and success of other acquisitions, if Branches would be an independent profit center or wrapped into a larger department, and would the management team (CEO, CFO, CTO) roles continue after acquisition.

In truth, Rebecca had many, many, many more questions about Huron and a potential acquisition. It was a completely foreign territory for her to be on this side of a transaction, and she didn't have a map. She took a picture of the whiteboard and then proceeded to create a running list of questions on her phone.

Over the next few days, anytime a question popped up, she wrote it down. Even if she had written it down before, she wrote it down again. Problem: awake at 3 A,M. with her brain refusing to shut off? Solution: write it all down. Just documenting her concerns somewhere let her feel a sense of control, and that she wasn't forgetting or neglecting anything.

"I think I need a code name."

"Like in a spy movie?" Richard was swirling a glass of cabernet, idly watching the legs drain to the bottom of the bell.

"Yeah, but not for me, for the project. I'm meeting with Don so much that people are starting to notice."

"Do you have to meet with him so often? Can you do longer meetings instead of frequent meetings? And is there really that much to prepare?"

Rebecca loved Richard, but sometimes he oversimplified problems. "Yeah, we've got most of the 'big' pieces nailed down as far as company specs. Now we're in the 'prep the presentation' stage. And we don't even know if I'll be giving a presentation. It might just be a hot seat where they pepper me with questions."

Richard waved his glass at her. "There's no question you can't answer about Branches. You know every line of code, every moving cog, every penny, and projection of that company."

"Hmm. But how to answer questions about those cogs and pennies without scaring them off or boring them to tears. Here, ask me something." She fished a stack of color-coded flash cards from her bag. The colors each represented what aspect of the business the question would cover. It helped her memory to have colors, it was just one of those things she did in elementary school and never stopped.

Richard looked at the impressive pile of cards and picked a pink one at random.

Pink meant it was a question about herself. There was a smattering of prompts in there, some softballs, some curveballs. The worst one was 'You don't seem to have any kind of enterprise technology background, why did you think you were qualified to start a tech company?' and it made her stammer every time. She silently prayed it wasn't that one.

"Tell us about yourself and how you came to start Branches."

"Well, I spent my corporate years implementing tech solutions for major companies, but I didn't enjoy how impersonal mega corporations were and how decisions and priorities were set. Plus, we were solving the same problem or a version of the same problem over and over and over again – it didn't make sense to me that there was not a comprehensive solution. So, I created Branches as a solution. It was a little scary to leave a cushy corporate job to become the boss, but I've had the support of my family, and so far, I'm proud of what we've accomplished."

Richard's face was ... not enthusiastic.

"What?"

"Don't admit you were scared to start Branches. Don't give them any reason to sense ANY weakness."

"I thought it would be humble and endearing."

"Nope. These are arrogant California tech bros. You're already a fish out of water being an east coast woman. You CANNOT give them more ammo by volunteering your fears."

"So, should I focus on my very generic computer science bachelor's degree I got from a state school before iPhones were invented? Maybe talk about my years as a corporate middle manager with no authority to make my own decisions?"

"I would completely ignore the part where they ask you about yourself. I'd dive into the problem you noticed first, then talk about your corporate contacts and experience as part of your start-up story. Then talk about yourself as CEO of Branches. That's all they need to know – you're the one at the top, making all the decisions."

"You see why I need these?" She snatched the card from Richard's hand and made a few notes on it. "I need to practice every single answer, not only so I know the answer, but how to best present that answer. It's a lot of work. A lot to remember."

"You're going to be fine."

"I don't even know how to talk about myself."

"I can tell this is going to be one of those conversations where I say positive things and you tell me I'm wrong."

Rebecca bit her lip.

"And now you're overthinking what you're about to say so I'm not right."

"Maybe."

"You're going to be fine." Richard stretched, as if he didn't have a care in the world.

Rebecca sighed. "With a lot of prep, yes, I'll be awesome. But in the meantime, I have a lot of work to do, a lot of meetings with Don, and a lot of people watching what I'm doing. There's only five more days before I fly out there, and I'm kinda freaking out."

"Tree."

"Tree?"

"Yes, your code name is 'Tree.'"

Rebecca tried to suppress a smile. "You're so lame."

"It's perfect, admit it."

"Never." She smirked then kissed him passionately.

Chapter Eighteen

THE HURON CAMPUS WAS A thirty-minute drive from the San Jose airport. The rideshare driver, seeing her destination, asked if she wanted the tech tour. Rebecca said sure, and he pointed out each of the exits and listed off the name brand companies as he made his way up the 101. It was a perfect distraction – every time her brain would want to run a simulation or a what if, or to remind her of that one time in middle school ... there was the driver saying, "That's where Google is"; "That's where Meta is"; "Have you heard of this obscure company?"; "Well, that's their exit coming up; "They'll be a household name next year ..."

Soon enough, Rebecca stood in front of the main entrance to Huron.

Her stomach was fluttering, and she triple checked that her bag still held her computer and back up thumb drive with a presentation she didn't know if she needed. As if it would disappear into a black hole when she was getting out the car. She shook her hair and wished she had checked a mirror at the airport. *Well, no helping it now.* Resolutely, she plastered on a smile and made her way to the reception desk.

The young man behind the counter smiled with perfect teeth. It was going to be a few minutes before they would be ready for her. Rebecca swiped her tongue subconsciously across her teeth. She really did need to take a beat and make sure she was ready for this meeting. It would be mortifying to lose a deal because her breakfast was stuck in her teeth.

The young man escorted her to the restroom and swiped her in. She hoped he didn't stand out there the whole time she was doing her business. The mirror above the sink revealed ... well, she looked like she just flew across the country for possibly the biggest meeting of her life.

A quick teeth-check and make-up refresh later, and she was left just staring at herself in the mirror. She met her own gaze. "You can do this." That seemed kind of weak when she said it out loud. She needed some other talisman but all she had was words. "You're a brilliant woman with a brilliant company and a brilliant future. They're going to see that and throw money at your feet. You can do this." She flushed, realizing she had said "you can do this" a second time, but it seemed right.

With nothing more to say, she straightened her posture and marched out for the biggest meeting of her life.

The young man was not waiting, and in fact was not at the front desk or in evidence at all when she made her way back to the lobby. Rebecca had the awkward, "did I just miss the bus feeling," but a few moments later, Calvin appeared and took her under his wing.

Even though she had only met him once, Rebecca felt relief that there was at least one familiar face in the building. He led her to a conference room where two men stood and shook her hand.

Alfred Cangro had a warm smile that crinkled his eyes and a neat trim of white hair around the crown of his bald spot. The CFO looked exactly like his company photo on Huron's website.

The CTO, Simon Liu, didn't make eye contact when he shook her hand; he seemed like many other brilliant but socially awkward engineers she had ever hired. In fact, she could easily picture him in a graphic t-shirt with some sort of nerdy joke or pun on it. So, it wasn't a surprise when he immediately jumped over small talk and asked, "Are you having difficulty getting customers to adapt to such a comprehensive and some might say complex solution? It seems like it's a big hurdle for adoption, and the message boards have a lot of loyalty for the classic more piecemeal approach."

Rebecca smiled and glanced at Alfred, who shrugged slightly. "It's been my experience that companies are in the market for secure, fast, comprehensive solutions and find the benefits of adopting Branches far outweighs the minor learning curve cost."

Simon nodded and opened his mouth to ask a follow-up question, but Calvin was quicker.

"Please." He gestured toward the table. "Let's sit and take a look at the agenda."

Simon nodded, amiable enough, and when they were seated, he slid the agenda over to her with a shy smile.

The agenda was unremarkably general:

- Overview

- Market

- Threats and Opportunities

- Financials

- Next Steps

After a few remarks about her flight and the weather, they were into the meat of the meeting.

"Tell us about yourself and how you came to start Branches? What problems are you attempting to solve?"

Rebecca couldn't believe her luck. She rattled off the polished answer she had worked on with Don and Richard. When she finished, she saw interest and approval and sat up a little straighter, feeling a little more confident that she could do this.

"Who are your top three competitors and how are you different?"

This also felt easy, for she knew her market space inside and out, and knew point for point where the similarities and differences were. The biggest struggle was to hold herself back from going overboard. If she wasn't careful, she'd end up spending twenty minutes answering just this one question.

"Does adopting Branches require companies to change how they do business today? Like a paradigm shift?"

She noted internally that this was basically what Simon had asked, and she wondered if there was a specific goal for adoption that they were trying to gauge. Or perhaps they were trying to overcome a similar hurdle.

"Tell me about your customers, you do have customers, right? Who are they, do they pay and what are they using this for?"

This one threw Rebecca a little. 'You do have customers, right?' was such a weird thing to say! *Are they trying to rattle me?* Testing to see if she'd break an NDA? And of course, her customers paid! She wasn't running a recipe blog funded by advertising views.

"Tell us about your team," required a small clarifying question; it wasn't one she had deliberately prepared for, and she wasn't sure if they wanted high-level answers or the current seating chart. And it turned out they wanted to know about her workforce (employee vs contractor) and their commitment level (she hired pros, not gig workers).

"Do you wish you could replace some of your team or are they good fits and belong on the Branches bus?"

She explained that she was a small company that couldn't afford to make bad hires. Everyone on the current team was a strong contributor and belonged on the bus. *I couldn't have done any of this without them*, she wanted to say, but refrained, worried it would make her sound weak.

"Walk us through your pipeline and use our metrics to characterize where you are in our terms?"

They handed Rebecca a flow chart, and after the briefest study, she did her best to judge her company against their matrix. This one she wasn't so sure she did well on, as Alfred frowned, and she wondered if she should have padded her answer a bit more.

That seemed to be the start of the "finance" questions, and pretty soon, she was feeling wrung out like a damp cloth. Why do they always talk money last in these kinds of meetings?

"Let's talk about your cash flow – are you keeping your head above water or are you bleeding cash?"; "How do you plan to grow the company with so little capital?"; "Your competitors are much better funded, why?"; "Have you raised any money?"; "If so, how much and how many investors do you have?"; "Would they consider another round or are they one and done?"; "Are you talking to any Venture Capital funds?"; "What's your plan B for keeping the doors open?"; "Do you have a plan C? ..."

It was all Rebecca could do to keep herself from going on the defensive.

The questions felt judgmental, and she struggled to keep "excuse words", such as "just" and "only", out of her answers. It was about this time that Simon excused himself. He was exceedingly polite but made it clear that his questions (the technical ones) had already been answered, and he had deadlines he needed to meet. Rebecca hoped that it was a good sign, but it didn't alleviate the feeling that she was being slowly roasted.

Alfred brought the firing squad portion of the meeting to a conclusion by asking, "What keeps you up at night? What are you afraid of?"

It pulled her up short. She looked at the table for a moment, wondering how honest she should be. "I worry about my family, mostly. That starting and running Branches puts them under strain they never asked for. I worry about my work family too, keeping them motivated and focused through the ups and downs. There are times both families keep going on faith, and I don't want to ever lose their faith in me."

Rebecca looked up to see Alfred smile; he seemed like he was a family man.

"Now I have a question for you. If I sell Branches to Huron, what are you planning to do with it? How does Branches fit into your overall plan?" It was a bit of a gamble, but the tone and tenor of the questions had led her to believe they were in the market for a purchase. Might as well get the cards on the table.

Calvin and Alfred shared a quick glance, and then Alfred took the reins. "Well, we have been looking for a solution like Branches for a while now. We considered building our own, but if there's a better solution in the marketplace, it may make sense to buy rather than build. As we have done our market research, it really looks like buying an existing solution will make more sense. Why reinvent the wheel? And right now, Branches is one of our top choices – but whatever we buy, Huron will integrate it into our products as part of our end-to-end services. This will help us differentiate ourselves from our competitors. We will also see it as a stand-alone offering similar to how you sell Branches today."

Rebecca nodded – this lined up with the research she had done in the last few weeks, but it was a relief that they were planning to keep Branches, not kill it as a competitor. "I imagine that Huron has a different culture and benefit package than just about every company you purchase. How would you rate Huron's success at integrating the disparate teams you acquire? What has worked and what has been a challenge?"

Alfred folded his hands, seemingly having to give this some thought. "I would give us a B minus," he then ventured. "Combining teams is hands-down the hardest part of an acquisition. Keeping the synergy and bringing it into the fold is a delicate dance. We're still learning what works and what doesn't. But that said, we know it's very important for everyone that we get it right. The biggest lesson we have learned is to have the CEO and others on the management team be an integral part of how we navigate these waters. You know your team, your culture, and together we can create a smooth transition. It's not always easy, but we believe it is worth the effort."

That felt like the most honest answer Rebecca could have hoped for. Change was hard on people, and she would have been suspicious if they claimed a spotless track record. "Will Branches remain its own profit center or will it become a piece of a larger department? In other words, how independent will it be?"

"Great question. The idea is that it's integrated into some of our legacy products, which would make us lean towards becoming part of a larger department. There's strong interest in also creating a Huron 'Lite' offering, which would leave Branches as a standalone profit center. So, I think we'll figure that out as we go."

Rebecca was torn about that one. She wanted Branches to be integrated so that there would be security for her team and her technology. But she built Branches out of her own need for independence. Letting it go was going to be hard no matter where they seated it within their hierarchy. "Assuming we move forward, would you be okay if I spoke with the CEOs of other companies you've already acquired? To get a sense of the experience?"

Calvin surprised her by jumping in. "Certainly, we can. However, there are some hoops we have to jump through first. Once we sign a term sheet, we'll send you the contact information for all the CEOs of our acquisitions over the past five years." He smiled reassuringly. "I'll let them know you might be reaching out, but these are busy people. I can't guarantee that they will respond to your request."

"I understand," Rebecca said. It was reasonable, but now she wanted to know what prerequisites came before the term sheet. But that wasn't the next question on her list. She decided to stick to her game plan. "How do you see the roles of the Branches management team evolving during the acquisition?"

Alfred stepped in again, saying, "Right now, the only thing I do know for sure is that Huron has a centralized CFO. So, if we do this deal, your CFO will exit within ninety days."

Don would be out. That would likely suit him just fine, as long as the payout was generous. Rebecca nodded thoughtfully, as if she was mulling this over rather than steeling herself for her big question. "How serious are you about actually acquiring us?"

Alfred looked her in the eyes and gave her a grandfatherly smile. "We're very serious about buying a company like Branches in the next ninety days."

Rebecca barely managed to stifle a gasp. A ninety-day acquisition was practically unheard of. She could feel her brain skip a beat.

Alfred was still talking "—help us decide who is the best acquisition for us. We'll be meeting with the board in two weeks to make our recommendation."

If they were going to move that fast, there had to be a lot more meetings like hers happening. She stuffed down her a confusing wave of excitement mixed with fear and attempted to keep her voice under control. "How much are you thinking of paying?"

"Probably less than you're thinking." Calvin smiled, turning on the charm. "It's really too early to go there. Let's figure out if we're the right fit for each other first."

Rebecca wondered if Calvin was trying to keep Alfred from giving away the game, or if he was just in charge of delivering bad news with a lot of charm.

"So, I guess my next question is the logistics of this thing. Let's say that

Branches is your top pick. What is happening in the next ninety days? What is your acquisition process like?"

"Well, I guess first, I need to preface this. We like to move quickly, but we also must be thorough. We've done acquisitions in sixty days, but we've also had deals take a year or more. In your case, you're a young company. I think we could do it in sixty to ninety days. We'll come to your office, spend two or three days reviewing your documents. You'll need to set aside a private workspace for us. All routine."

"Okay, going back to my question about contacting reference CEOs ... You said we'd need to have a term sheet signed first. When does that happen in your order of operations?"

———

Rebecca sat in the Admiral Club lounge at SFO. The meeting had run so long that her flight had departed from San Jose airport before she had left the conference room. At one point she had looked up, startled to realize the sun was going down. Calvin had called the company travel agent and gotten her rebooked, and graciously called the rideshare on Huron's account as well. She was more grateful than she could admit for that kindness.

It was so strange. She might be within ninety days of a windfall of money, and she could hardly afford a cab ride through Bay Area traffic. It would be bearable if the deal was a guarantee, but they wouldn't even confirm Branches would be their "pick" to purchase. The conversation had been filled with too many "ifs," and they had hedged on every answer. She could be ninety days from nothing but more bills and the feeling of the Sisyphean task of preventing her ship from sinking.

Rebecca had managed to get them to outline their purchase process, and it was more complicated than she had imagined. First, they were going to pick the target company and present it to their board. If the board agreed, they would begin their due diligence. If they picked Branches, the first she would hear of any of this was when they reached out to have her sign a "no shop" agreement, and she'd have to cease acquisition conversations she was having with any other companies (*haha!*) for sixty days.

After that, they'd come visiting. It was like a weird courtship process, where they'd figure out if they liked Branches enough to put a contract on it. Huron's people would be poking around her offices and combing through her books. At that point they might say yes, they might say no.

If they finished going through all her undergarments and wanted to proceed, then they'd start talking money. She had asked how Huron came up with their number and they gave her a bit of mumbo jumbo about an algorithm. She very much doubted it was all computers spitting out completely impartial valuations. In fact, it appeared there'd be some expectation that Branches would come up with their own number and then they'd begin negotiations to close the gap.

Once all that was settled, then Rebecca would meet with their CEO to finalize the price. She checked her notes, his name was Raymond Gomez and he'd been with Huron for five years. Once they met eye to eye and agreed on a number, a term sheet would be signed, and she would finally be able to talk to other CEOs about their acquisition experience. She'd have to find out something pretty horrific to decide to back out at that point. But even the term sheet wasn't binding. It seemed like the whole thing could fall apart at any point until the ink dried on the final contract and the check cleared.

Part of her wanted to walk away now. This was going to be stressful and distracting and would actually cost her money and time in the short term. And no matter what, she'd have to keep the company solvent and growing through the entire process.

Rebecca felt like she was getting a headache just looking at all her notes. Why was she even considering this? Should she be considering this? Could she even make this decision herself? With a sinking feeling she realized she couldn't. Not really. She wrote "Board of Directors Meeting!" on her to-do list.

"Hey, Branches."

Rebecca jerked in surprise. Standing in front of her was a familiar man, somewhat arrogant and definitely annoyed. She had been concentrating so much, she had the feeling she had missed him greeting her a few times. Where did she know him from?

And then it clicked.

"Hello, Octopus."

"Brent," he corrected with a tight smile.

"Rebecca."

"You headed to the Tech and Digital Innovations thing? I didn't see your name on the speaker list."

Rebecca smiled. "No, I'm homeward bound."

"Yeah, I didn't think that was going to be your scene."

Rebecca became aware that all her notes from her meeting were spread out in front of her. All Brent had to do was look down. "Really, so what do think my scene is?" She casually began shuffling the pages, picking them up into a pile, like she was nervous.

"Medical tech, right? No extra networking or chumming about. Very directed, purpose-driven conferences with target markets only."

"I'm flattered, I didn't realize Branches was on your radar."

"Oh, I keep my eye out; you have to do that if you want to stay on top."

Rebecca nodded, giving a polite smile again. "Well, I wish you luck at your conference."

Brent seemed annoyed, like she wasn't reading from the same script he was. He looked at her like a high school bully searching for where to stick a dagger. "Did you know we've picked up a couple of your employees? They seem pretty happy with more pay and stability."

Rebecca now had to force a tight smile. "I'm glad to hear Jonathan is doing well. Give him my best." She stood and gathered her bags. "Again, best of luck at your conference, but I believe my flight is boarding."

She walked out of the lounge with a straight back.

By the time she made it to the gate, she was giggling hysterically. Between Huron and Octopus, it had been a rollercoaster of a day, and she took a beat to get her emotions back on an even keel. She didn't want to be *that* crazy person on the airplane. And as she stood there, taking deep breaths, and grinning madly, it finally clicked. Even though she had no idea what was to come about with Huron, her confidence in the viability of Branches had soared. Brent thought he knew her tiny little company and was lording Jonathan over her? How could she have ever been worried about a clown like that? She was still grinning as she boarded the plane for home.

Chapter Nineteen

"HOW IS THE SALES FUNNEL?" Don asked hopefully.

They were reviewing the month-to-date numbers, and they were ... bleak. Expenses were still outstripping income, but the gap was narrowing.

"Anything likely to close before payroll?"

"Nothing definitive. There's a few out there circling, but it's so hard to tell when they'll land." Rebecca admitted.

"Well, we've got the cash to make payroll this round, but I don't know how we can make a hire, never mind two. Not without making a perilous situation untenable," Don said.

"Yeah." Rebecca sighed. "I was thinking about it too. I don't think we should fill Jonathan's position. Just gaps with a contractor until the picture changes."

"And the new salesperson?"

"I don't see how we can get around it." Rebecca waved a hand towards her laptop, "I'm bringing in new leads to pump up the pipeline. If we're going to have a chance at landing them, they can't wait three weeks for a spot on my calendar. We need a dedicated salesperson to follow up on calls, chase down leads, and close deals."

"Do you have a candidate in mind yet? We need someone with a track record for closing high-dollar sales. If they can't do it, the sunk costs might sink us."

Rebecca sat back in her chair. "Well, I wanted to run this past you, see how the money would look. What if instead of hiring someone on salary, I hire a salesperson to work commission?"

Don nodded. "Like, they sell your product, they get a percentage? Or they get a flat rate?"

"The best salespeople would want a percentage. And I need the best." Rebecca smiled brightly at him.

"We'd have to look at our state laws, employee manual, insurance, all that kind of stuff to make sure that we're covered for that kind of position."

Rebecca wrinkled her nose. "Crap. I hadn't thought about that part of it. I keep thinking I don't want to bankrupt the company by giving too high of a commission, but it needs to have the possibility of a strong income, or we won't attract the right candidates. What would the commission rate need to be to strike that balance?"

"I'd have to run some numbers." Don squinted briefly at the ceiling, "How many deals would you expect them to close in a month?"

"I've been averaging one a week."

"So, after they're fully trained, you'd want them to do that level of sales or higher?" Don asked.

"Can I say higher? I'd love it to be higher."

"We could do a bonus for extra sales in a month."

"Oh, that sounds exciting." Rebecca smiled. "It would attract the thrill of the kill type. But I do have to ask: any idea how it will look to Huron if they show up next week to inspect the books?"

"I don't know if we should consider them. It's been three weeks, and you haven't heard from them, have you?"

It was true. The first few days after coming back from California had been a flurry of excitement. She had texted the entire odyssey to Richard before she got home, and he'd run out to buy a bottle of champagne to toast her success. Don had been in her office first thing the next day for the full debrief. She'd called a meeting of the Board of Directors and filled them in on the whole trip, why Huron was interested and the next steps. There had been a stunned silence followed by a palpable appreciation for the possible sale.

Only Arun had been unhappy with the turn of events. Not that he objected to possibly selling his interest in the company at a profit, but that she didn't clear the meeting with the board prior to having it. Louise was the surprise voice of reason to quickly jump in and point out that it would be entirely ineffective to have Rebecca clear her schedule with the board, and as an entrepreneur, Rebecca needed the flexibility to explore opportunities for the company. She was bringing the opportunity to the board, which is what she was supposed to do. Arun grumbled a bit before bowing to the logic of this.

The board made her promise to keep them informed, and then … nothing. The phone had not rung once, not with a "no thanks" or a "you're still in consideration." The absolute silence from Huron was deafening. But the board had been reaching out to her for updates. She'd been upbeat, but now she was facing the reality that this was going to go nowhere, and everyone was going to be disappointed.

"I'm beginning to wonder if they'll just completely ghost us. We may never know anything."

"Maybe," Don said. "But also, these kinds of companies have all the time in the world. In the meantime, we have to keep the lights on, and the desks staffed."

"So, you think I should hire someone on commission, and if it scuppers the deal later, oh well?"

"I'm a pragmatist, Rebecca." Don spread his hands palms up, bobbing them like he was juggling. "We have to make payroll." His left hand dipped with the weight of payroll. "We may have to justify shifting future income to fulfill present needs." The right hand tipped a tiny bit.

Rebecca nodded. "Payroll wins. Okay, I'll have Laura run the ad for the position as a commission-based role."

"Sounds good. And, if this month is a loss, we may need to look at tightening the belt a little bit more around here. Maybe let go of employees in favor of contractors."

"Ugh, I really don't want to cut staff."

"I know. We'll keep trying to make it work. But it has to be at least on the table."

"Okay," Rebecca agreed. "I'll also see if any of the investors want to double down in the meantime. I've got a dinner meeting with Louise tonight. I think she wants to talk me off the ledge."

The restaurant was tastefully decorated and had a lovely aroma of garlic and basil.

Louise was waiting at a table with a bottle of red and two glasses. "I don't mind the corkage fee," Louise explained. "I picked up a case when I was in Napa last year, and I just love it so much. You really have to taste it."

Rebecca had shown up to dinner ready to defend, explain, and otherwise justify her decisions. However, over the course of the next hour, Louise didn't mention Branches once. In fact, she seemed to deliberately steer the conversation away from anything work related, asking about Rebecca's family, talking about travel, and laughing over their mutual attempts at wine and paint nights.

Rebecca felt the conversation and the wine, slowly but surely, unwinding her anxiety. For the first time in a while, she realized she felt seen as a human being, not just a CEO, and it was lovely.

Surveying the empty plates, Rebecca sighed. "Thank you for this. I don't think I realized how much I needed it."

"I've been there. When I was selling my company, I was a wreck for months. It is stressful, and you have to take time for self-care."

"I just wish they would call. Let me know if they've gone a different way, or whatever. The waiting is miserable."

"How long has it been?"

"Three weeks."

"Hm." Louise smiled at her. "It's not like dating, you know, you're actually allowed to call them."

"What?"

"Call them and check in. Ask if they've made a recommendation to the board yet. If they've picked another company, they'll tell you. If you're still in the running, they'll tell you. Silence just means they're busy. They seemed like busy people, right?"

"Yeah."

"It's not unreasonable to call for an update."

"Okay." Rebecca was surprised at the feeling in her gut, the resistance to calling Huron, to knowing for sure, felt enormous.

Louise gave her an inscrutable look. "It's scary either way. But it's torture not to know."

"Am I that easy to read?"

"No, but I remember what it was like."

"I am so lucky. I had no idea when we met that I'd even consider selling my company. And here you are, with all the experience I need, right when I need it. And you are being so generous with that knowledge. I want you to know how much I appreciate it."

Louise picked up her mostly empty glass in salute. "You've got this, Rebecca."

———

Huron had always initiated contact, so Rebecca was a little taken aback when she couldn't reach a human. The night before, Richard had role-played all the worst-case scenarios with her, so she would be prepared for rejection, disappointment, and any form of humiliation she could imagine. She had spent her morning shower time prepping what she was going to say and how she was going to charm the secretary and be connected with Calvin for a status update. After all that build up, having no option to speak to a person was so awkward that she hung up instead of leaving a message.

A full day at the office later, it occurred to her that maybe the "no human" option was because she called before west coast office hours.

Rebecca tried back, and again got the same recorded options, but this time she was prepared to leave a message. "Hello, this is Rebecca Hoffman from Branches. I came out to your office about a month ago to meet with Calvin, Simon, and Alfred about a possible collaboration between our companies ... or an acquisition. Anyway, it's been a few weeks, and I haven't heard any updates. So, I'm calling for ... uh, updates." She hastily left her contact information and hung up.

Gah! This is so nerve wracking! She jumped up and down in her office, flicking her arms like she was trying to shake off water.

Laura poked her head in. "Everything okay in here?"

"Yeah. Just trying to get out some yuckiness." Rebecca reflected for a moment on how strange that might sound. "My daughter would declare a dance party to shake it out."

"Your daughter sounds fun."

"She is. Parenting isn't easy, but sometimes they surprise you. Like declaring a dance party and they're right. You can't feel the same after three minutes of dancing."

"Same. What's your go-to song?"

Rebecca drew a blank. "Hm. I think Tori must always chose."

"Well, if you have a minute for it, can we talk TNT?"

"Oh, sure." Rebecca realized that she hadn't been paying much attention to Laura's project at all. She felt guilty as they sat down to review the program.

"Well, I think the long and short of it," Laura said, "is that TNT has gone as far as it can without actually building it. In the beginning, it was on the development schedule, but it fell off, and no one seems to know when it's getting added back in."

"Okay, remind me, what was the last message to the interest list?"

"About a month ago, teasing features and benefits, pretty much the same stuff I've been sending out. The content's been going stale, and people are opting out."

Rebecca frowned. "I know you're not going to want to hear this, Laura, but I think we're going to have to stop TNT plans." She felt bad about the decision – between the Branches testing debacle and the cancelation of TNT, it was two big blows to Laura. "This isn't a reflection on you and your work. It's more of my fault for going down this path in the first place.

It was a distraction, and I should have kept 100 percent of my resources on Branches' core product."

Laura visibly deflated. "There's not ... I didn't ..."

"Hey, this is a business decision, not a personal one, and it wouldn't matter if you had done backflips down the hallway. We need every programmer to work on Branches."

Laura nodded at the table.

"I need you to look at me," Rebecca said, hearing the echo of what she said it to Tori behind the hostess stand.

Laura met her eyes, and Rebecca noticed there were tears threatening to fall. She dug out a box of tissues and passed them over with a reassuring smile, "You and I are okay. Okay?"

Laura nodded, still a little too emotional to trust her own voice.

"Here's how we're going to do this and save face. I need you to send out an email to the list and say that 'we received an unexpected response to our special beta invitation, and we are booked,' and then say we'll follow up in a few months."

"But we never sent out a special beta invitation."

Rebecca waved the concern away. "These people receive well over 100 emails a day, the worst that will happen is someone says, 'hey, I missed the beta Invite, what gives?' and we say, 'oh there must have been a delivery issue. We'll let you know when it opens again in a few months.'"

"What do we say in a few months?"

"I think in a few months it will drop off the radar entirely." Rebecca crossed her fingers beneath her desk. Laura, however, seemed hesitant, and Rebecca didn't blame her. She'd need something else to do now, at least in the short term to keep her confidence. And in fact, there was a project ...

"Speaking of the coming months, there might be a special project coming up, and I'll need your help to prep. If it happens, it'll be on short notice, so I want to have as much planned as possible."

"What kind of project is it?"

Rebecca smiled. "Not a TNT kind of project, if that's what you're asking. But first things first, I need you to check with building management for a private office space in the building. If this project happens, there'll be three to five people working there for about a month and we'll need to be able to securely store paperwork in the room. Can you find out if there are any spaces like that available at not-too-steep of a price? You're good at that."

"Sure." Laura seemed to perk up.

"And if they happen to have a spare lockable file cabinet around, snag it."

"I know exactly where to find it," Laura said, her confidence clearly rebounding.

Rebecca was glad that Laura seemed to have recovered without shedding a tear. She really did have a bright future ahead of her.

———

The new salesperson oozed confidence into the telephone. Rebecca could just imagine all the concerns of the potential buyer melting away on the other side of the line. Jerome had picked up on the Branches' selling points right away, and now, almost at the end of the two-week training cycle, he was inventing his own ways to overcome objections. She had given him a list of cans and can nots, and he was navigating it with aplomb.

Rebecca wondered why she had been so hesitant to hire a salesperson. True, she had almost had an aneurism the first time she had let him take the lead on a sales call. She wondered if that made her a control freak. But he had landed a sale in his first week and, judging by the way this call was progressing, he likely would have another notch in his belt this week. When she handled the sales, one a week was the most she could expect. It was obvious now that Jerome could handle more volume, and her next big jump was just a matter of adding quality leads into the pipeline.

Guessing that lead generation wouldn't take as much time as all the sales meetings, Rebecca dared to think what new initiatives she could spearhead with the new-found freedom. *Perhaps—*

Rebecca's cell screen lit up with an incoming call followed by a silly ringtone Tori had put on her phone. She barely had time to register a California number before she slapped it to voicemail. She looked over at Jerome apologetically. He winked back and made a gesture to say it would be okay to call them back. Rebecca glanced at the California number. It had been over a month since her trip to the Bay Area to meet with Huron. She had left her second voicemail last week, and this week she had dug out the email of the executive assistant and given that a try.

It was almost too much to hope that this was the call, but she had given them her personal cell. A voicemail notification popped up and the phone was to her ear in the next instant.

"Hi, Rebecca, this is Vince, I'm the desk assistant at Huron. I want to apologize, as it wasn't until I got your email that I realized I had missed your voicemail. I'm following up with the team now to see what the latest developments are. I should have an update for you in the next day or so. Again, sorry to leave you hanging, please email me again if you have any additional questions."

Her heart was beating so fast that she played it a second time to make sure she understood.

Hmmm. So, no definitive answers, but I've climbed out of the void.

She didn't think for a moment that her voicemails had gone nowhere. They likely were keeping her in the dark on purpose until they had a definitive yes or no, and she was getting a response now because they were close to making a decision. That was progress at least, even if it was out of her control.

Jerome was giving her an "is everything okay?" look as he continued his call. "Can I clarify, are you asking if there is a discount for purchasing the whole year up front?"

She smiled at him and nodded. "Yes, that's something that we can do." She hastily wrote down a number for him, and he relayed the information smoothly, as if he knew it the whole time. He was going to land this sale. She couldn't help thinking it was an omen.

Chapter Twenty

---◆---

THE CALL CAME THE FOLLOWING afternoon. Rebecca's heart did a backflip the second her cellphone screen illuminated with the California number. She took a deep breath and released it slowly. "Hello?"

"Hi, Rebecca? This is Calvin from Huron."

"Hi Calvin, so good to hear from you."

"Uh, yes, I know it's been a while, and I appreciate your patience. How are things going out there?"

"Good, good. I've got a new salesperson who is absolutely killing it."

"Congrats! I saw that you had a sold-out beta product, too?"

"Oh wow, I didn't realize you were on that list!"

"Of course, we are." She could hear Calvin smiling on the other end of the line. "We like to keep tabs on all the companies we're interested in acquiring."

Rebecca wasn't sure what to say, so she didn't say anything.

"You there?" Calvin asked.

"Yes, just wondering if you're still interested in acquiring Branches."

"Well, the short answer is yes. We had it narrowed down to two companies, and yours is the one we presented to the board. If you're still interested in exploring this purchase with us, we'd like to move forward."

Rebecca pressed the heel of her palm to her sternum and massaged her palpating heart. This whole journey was going to kill her. "Yes. Yes, I'm still interested."

"Excellent. I'm going to forward you a timeline and package. You'll want to review it with your team and prepare all the required documents before anyone from Huron comes out there. Do you think that'll be a problem?"

"I don't think so, but I guess it will depend on when I see the list."

"Oh, yeah. Good point. I'll hit send on this email, and then let's have a call early next week. How does Monday afternoon, your time work?"

"I'll clear my schedule," Rebecca said, trying to effuse her voice with a warm smile. "I look forward to talking to you then."

A few moments later he rang off, and Rebecca wasn't sure what to do. Her body was jittery with adrenaline, and she wanted to jump up and down. She settled for a quick elevator downstairs to call her husband and share her victory.

———

The "package" had sounded innocuous enough. But Rebecca couldn't seem to get her brain to focus on it. She got to the third bullet point and found herself scrolling, scrolling, scrolling to the bottom. There were 141 items on the company due diligence list, and a whole separate and equally long list of items just for the code Branches had developed.

If it was just Rebecca, and no one else, she'd throw her hands up in despair. She didn't know where a third of these items were, and there were a good number of items on the list that didn't seem to be written in English at all. She needed a business-ese translator.

Luckily for her, she had a team!

The office space Laura had found was two floors up from Branches, a no-man's land buffering two larger companies, but it was too small to be worth absorbing into any particular workspace. It was just large enough to accommodate a locking filing cabinet, a round table, a few chairs, and the people to fill it. Without knowing the length of time, she would need this space, Laura had done a remarkably good job negotiating a fair rate for the space.

Laura was already there when Don and Rebecca arrived. On Rebecca's company calendar it said: "Lunch with Don," and technically that was true. It was just also including Laura and a pizza delivery.

Between bites of piping hot pizza, Rebecca read Laura in on the possible acquisition.

"That sounds really cool, but like, what does it mean?" Laura asked.

Rebecca cocked her head. "For the company? If it succeeds, Branches will have access to way more resources, leads and an industry-recognized brand. It will basically take Branches from a mom-and-pop shop to an international player."

"Okay," Laura said, her voice not sounding sure at all.

"The code name for all of this while we discuss it further is going to be 'Tree,' so anything acquisition related on our calendars should have that label."

"Got it." This time Laura sounded much surer of herself.

"And this must remain confidential. You *cannot* discuss it with anyone outside of this room, whether they work at Branches or not. In fact, one of the first items on this list is for us all to sign a nondisclosure agreement."

Rebecca slid the files out of her binder and passed them over to Don and Laura.

Don didn't bother to read, just signed. Laura bit her lip, scanning through the paperwork. She glanced up, saw Don had signed and then quickly did the same.

The rest of the meeting was used to go line-by-line through the list, translating it into plain English and divvying up responsibilities. At the end of the meeting, they each had a smaller, slightly more manageable list to tackle. They agreed to meet again in three days.

"I can't believe they won't accept a digital signature. What decade are they doing business in?"

To Rebecca's frustration, the selling process revealed her greatest weakness: filing. Every day was a variation of: "where is this document?" And if she happened to find the correct document, it became a hunt for reasons why the document may or may not be acceptable. For example, the employee documents were fine for digital signatures, but the NDAs needed wet signatures. Laura had gamely printed off NDAs and charmed the staff into resigning in ink. *Bless her.* But that was just one instance of roughly ten billion documents her little company was supposed to have at their fingertips.

Thankfully, the Huron admin, Vince, had allowed them to put his direct number on speed dial. He'd been a complete champ helping them sort through the acceptable/unacceptable forms of paperwork. If he was doing this for every company Huron was acquiring, it suddenly made sense how her pre-acquisition phone calls had slipped through the cracks. The man was busy.

So was Laura. Rebecca kept sending her lists of things she couldn't find. And Laura would dutifully search and fish the documents out of the database like a miracle. Or it absolutely didn't exist anywhere, and they would have to add it to an ongoing list of things to chase down and resign. Like the office space lease. That one still bugged her. She knew it was in a yellow folder ... somewhere. One day, she'd be clearing out her desk, or her home office, and it would no doubt pop up and bite her. But in the meantime, Laura had trudged up to management and gotten fresh copies of everything.

It was official. She was going to have to give Laura a bonus, because the sale, if it ever proceeded, would be due to Laura doing all the grunt work. She jotted down Travis' name as well. And then she considered the people who had so generously made introductions. Her networking group, her former colleagues, and most especially, the airport squad. There would be no way she could throw money at all of them, and in some cases, it would be weird and inappropriate. But she did want to express her gratitude ... somehow.

Speaking of. She was due to meet with Don in the "Tree office" to discuss employee benefits, how they would be affected by the acquisition, and how to communicate that to Huron.

There was a brief knock at her door before Rodney poked his head in. "Hey, I was hoping to catch you before lunch."

"Sure, what's going on?"

"Well, I'll be quick. Uh ..." Rodney's face strained with the effort of summarizing the issue in his head. "Bottom line, how important is the commenting of the code? Where does it fit in our priorities?"

"I take it that this isn't something we've been doing as we go then."

"No." He looked down in embarrassment. "I haven't been doing it like I should. I did a quick spot check, and the rest of the team has been leaving comments to keep their train of thought from one day to the next, not this is where this section of code does commentary. Bao seems to be leaving consistent comments in her code, but it's all in Chinese. I'd have to sit down with the dictionary to figure out if they're personal notes or what."

Rebecca leaned her elbows on the table and rubbed her fingers on her forehead.

Rodney spoke into the silence, "I take it that this is a priority, then."

It was. It was the most daunting portion of the entire technology checklist. And they were at square one. And her team had a full plate just keeping up with the current workload. She was going to have to hire someone to go in and comment out the code.

"Any idea how big an effort it would be to get someone in to add the comments?" Rebecca asked.

Rodney squinted at the ceiling for a moment. "Well, I'm not sure. But everyone needs to do their own. We can do it as we create the code, but it'll impact our schedule." He clearly did a little mental math and then offered, "Maybe set things back a week or more?"

Rebecca groaned. "Okay, let's do this. Let's go back to doing code walkthroughs like we did in the very early days – that will force commenting to happen. We'll do a walkthrough from a milestone about a month back, and then let's do them regularly. The early code that's not commented, we'll figure out later, but this will make the shift we need. Sound good?"

"And when they push back?"

"Remind them that walkthroughs we were always part of their job description."

Rodney gave her an appraising look. "There are a few reasons I can think of why this would be a big priority."

Rebecca smiled; Rodney was no fool. But she also couldn't disclose the acquisition to him directly. "In your experience, are they good reasons?"

"Mostly, yes."

Rebecca let her smile broaden.

Rodney smile answered hers. He cleared his throat. "Well, then. Are there any other code concerns I can get on top of for you?"

"At the moment, I'm good, but I may run a few things by you for accuracy."

"I'm here when you need me."

Bless that man. She'd have to add him to the bonus list too.

———

The employees' files were fanned out on the table. Half were annotated with sticky notes tallying stock options and benefits. But the problem was, she wasn't sure they were accurate. Like Rodney. At some point, she bonused him with stock options. But was that already included in his employee file total? The details were fuzzy. She could verify a balance change, if she could just remember why she had bonused him in the first place. When he had jumped in to fill the void after Jonathan quit? Or was that when they were still doing freelance work for Lindsey?

She sighed, scrawling a giant question mark on a sticky note, and slapping it to the file.

Don looked up from the file he was reviewing. "You, okay?"

"Yeah, I'm just going to be searching Slack for all mentions for stock, options, and bonuses going back to the beginning of time. And I just realized there are some former employees that were bonused stock too. I don't think I've seen Jonathan's file yet."

Don rolled his eyes. "That guy."

"Yeah, according to Laura, he's already looking for the exit at Octopus."

"She's still in contact with him?"

Rebecca shrugged. "He emailed to let her know there might be an employment history verification. She got the feeling he was trying to see if the bridge was burned."

"Is there anyone else out there with stock to claim?"

"I don't think so."

"No, 'an artist who drew a mural and I paid them in stock' scenarios." Don cocked a quizzical eyebrow.

"That was Zuckerberg, right?"

"Yeah," Don confirmed.

"No, to be honest, I wasn't sure I'd ever sell. And I wasn't sure if the company was even going to survive. It didn't feel right to pay people in promises."

Don grinned. "It worked out alright for the Facebook artist."

Rebecca raised an eyebrow and then shrugged in surrender. "I think that's the exception that proves the rule."

"I don't think that Huron will pay out the stock upfront to employees," Don said.

"What do you mean?"

"Well," Don assumed what Rebecca mentally called 'teacher mode' and settled back into his chair. "If you had a sudden windfall just as your company was going through a major transition, would you stay on? Or would you take the money and cash in a few months or years to figure out what you want to do next?"

"Okay, I see the point, it's fair," Rebecca conceded. "But we can't just not pay them though."

"No, we'll have to escrow some of the money from the sale and hold it for a while to incentivized employees to stay through the transition. I've seen deals for a year or two, never much longer than that."

Rebecca drummed her fingers on the table, thinking. "So, they get a partial payment upfront and a full payout at the end of the transition period."

"Probably. Have you had a chance to look at their benefit package versus ours?"

"Yeah, for the most part theirs is superior." Rebecca smiled ruefully. "Some employees are going to be upset that they have to change health insurance. But they have a 401(k) with match, bank holidays off, and an extra week of vacation. It's the kind of package I would want if I were them."

"I have the revised expense and revenue projections for you." Don slid the paperwork across the table.

Rebecca eyed the documents dubiously. "You know, I used to have a boss that printed everything. Every darn thing, she'd even print emails. And it was just so ridiculous that she couldn't function with a screen. And now here I am, needing a whole separate office for confidential paperwork."

"Life has a funny way of making you put the shoe on the other foot."

"I guess so." Rebecca reached for the projections. "Anything I should really pay attention to here?"

"The expense projections should be dead-on. Depending on billing cycles, it fluctuates by ten thousand dollars or so, but for a company this size, that's pretty dialed in. The revenue side could use your attention. It is, uh, optimistic."

"Too optimistic? Or justifiably optimistic?" Rebecca flipped through the pages. "Oh, yeah. That's optimistic. How did you come to it?"

"We've been holding fairly consistently for a while now on leads turning into prospects, and our conversion rate is trending upward. So, I projected that we'd invest in more lead generation."

"Without a drop off in the quality of leads? That sounds like a neat trick."

Don shrugged, sheepishly. "If they buy Branches, they can bring their own extensive contacts into the pipeline and none of it will matter anyway."

Rebecca considered. "Well, if we don't sell, I'll need to come up with a new lead generation strategy. I'll frame up something for it."

"Within our current budget, preferably," Don replied. "We need to stay completely solid on the expense side. They're going to be looking at worse-case scenario … What will they have to fund themselves."

"Okay," Rebecca agreed. "And I'm sure it has nothing to do with not wanting to redo all of your hard work so far."

Don smiled. "Nothing at all."

Chapter Twenty-One

"THEY'RE HERE," LAURA SAID IN an exaggerated whisper as she shut Rebecca's office door behind her.

Rebecca's stomach gave a nervous flutter. "Here, here? Or upstairs here?"

"Upstairs here. Three of them."

Rebecca let go of a breath she hadn't realized she was holding. Things hadn't been trucking along as quickly as the original timeline had indicated. It had taken a while before they had even made their decision to proceed, and the documentation part on her side had taken longer than expected as well. But this part, the office visit? It had materialized faster than she anticipated.

If the due diligence team stuck to their agenda, they would be upstairs reviewing all the documents today, and tomorrow would be a review of Branches' code. They shouldn't be visiting the office itself, as that would stir up too many questions and potentially kill the deal. But part of her still feared they would show up and want to shake hands with every programmer in the bullpen. That would be a disaster.

Rebecca's eyes flitted to the ceiling as if she had x-ray vision. "Did you offer them coffee or something to eat?"

"Yes, they're all set. And I confirmed the caterer for lunch."

Rebecca nodded thoughtfully. "Thank you."

Laura lingered. "Can I ask you something?"

There was a nervous note in her voice that caught Rebecca's attention down from her inspection of the ceiling. "Sure. What's up?"

"Well, if the company sells, what happens to us?"

"Us?"

"Yeah. The team."

"Well, if Huron was interested in buying Branches just to shut us down, I wouldn't be considering an offer. So, Branches will continue on." However, judging by Laura's wide eyes, closing Branches had never even occurred to her. So, her concern must be about ... "Are you asking about the people who work here?" Rebecca clarified.

Laura nodded.

"The vast majority of the employees will keep their jobs, have greater security, and access to more benefits. There's going to be a transition time as Huron takes over, and some of the team may decide to go. But the only department for sure that's on the block is finance. Huron has their own financial team."

Laura's eyebrows raised and then furrowed as she clearly worked through the implications. "So, Don is working on this merger, but he'll be out of a job?"

"He'll be well compensated for it, and his value will go up from the experience. The next 'Branches' to hire him will have to pay more."

"And me?" There was a tremor in her voice.

Rebecca felt like an idiot. Laura was asking about her own job – not everyone else's.

"Here's the thing," Rebecca said. "Branches is always going to need someone to caretake the geniuses that work here. You do that admirably, making sure there's office supplies and food and keeping me organized on a day-to-day basis. The job is secure. However, you're more than this job. You're going to grow and develop more skills and seek out new challenges. And we'll be happy for you when that day comes – and I do think it's coming quicker than you realize. You're graduating soon, aren't you?"

"Next spring, yeah."

"And have you given any thought to what you're going to do after that?"

"I ... I'm not really sure. There's just so many choices, you know?"

"Yes. I know that feeling." Rebecca remembered that feeling all too well. And she realized with a start that she had the perfect way to thank her for all her hard work and support with Branches. "Tell you what. When this whole thing calms down a bit, let's have a talk. Call it career counseling plus, okay?"

"Really?"

"Yeah, of course. You've got a bright future, Laura."

Laura flushed. "Thank you, I appreciate that."

The due diligence team from Huron had been great and easy to work with, yet they were somewhat buttoned up. It was their third meeting in two days, and Rebecca still wasn't sure what to make of the whole ordeal.

On the second day, they had presented her with a checklist of mostly completed items they had reviewed the day before. She clarified and provided additional documentation, answering questions about the majority of the outstanding items. They then proceeded to go over the company financials, predictably questioning the projections. The team had seemed to agree with Don's expenses, as they hadn't really asked any follow-ups to those numbers. Rebecca had prepared extensively on the projections and felt that her confidence and willingness to go as deep into the numbers as they wished worked in her favor. If they were testing for weak spots, they didn't seem to find one there.

Her spidey senses tingled towards the end of the meeting. When she got back to her desk, she realized they didn't ask about or even mention the lack of comment on the code. It didn't feel like something they would miss. It felt like it might be a giant elephant in the room that could squash the deal in silence.

Rebecca pulled up slack and pinged Rodney. *Available for a confidential walk around the block?*

Three dots flashed as he typed his reply. *Do I get to know what Tree is?*

Rodney was sharp as a tack. She smiled. *Tree's definitely come with fresh air. Let's walk.*

Meet you downstairs in 5.

On the street, she sized him up quickly. Rodney was unshaven and wearing a graphic t-shirt with a computer science joke on it. Not remotely dressed to meet someone outside the company, but what the hell, at least his hair was clean. He was the genius behind the code; maybe they were used to eccentric types. She quickly filled him in on the acquisition and the team pawing through the company documents in the name of due diligence.

"They're upstairs right now?" Rodney glanced up at the building as if they were looking down on him at that moment.

"Yeah. And I need you to be ready to meet them. Answer their questions and talk about the status of the code commenting."

"Geez. Couldn't you have given me just a little bit of notice?"

"Yeah, I could have. But you're great on the fly, I've seen it. I know you can do this."

In truth, she had never seen him communicate with anyone outside of the company about Branches. Rodney did know the code front and back, was part of every decision along the way, and sometimes completely lost her when explaining issues. But to explain it to outsiders? She was asking him for a Hail Mary here, and to her surprise, he seemed to think he could do it.

———

Less than an hour later, Rodney sat at the table, and she was viscerally reminded of his job interview. The confidence just oozed out of him, she wanted to hire him all over again. And wow – did he know how to talk about the code to non-programmers? Absolutely.

Rodney was honest and knowledgeable as he took them through the paces. When the commenting came up, he explained it had fallen off when deadlines were tight. He said it with such charm that the due diligence team actually laughed it off.

Rebecca thought she might die of relief.

And now here they were. Two hours later and the team was packing up their bags, getting ready to head back to California.

Rebecca wasn't sure how to ask it. Wasn't even sure if she wanted to know the answer. But ... "So, what's next?"

The one woman on the team looked up and smiled, but it was the older gentleman who answered.

"We're going to recommend that Huron makes an official offer to purchase Branches."

"Wow. Really?" Rebecca could have kicked herself for sounding so surprised.

"Really. Congratulations."

Rebecca shook the hand he offered. "Thank you."

The woman produced a document from a manila folder. "This is the official letter of recommendation and an outline of the next steps in the process. We'll also send a digital copy to you and your attorney. Calvin will be in touch to negotiate numbers."

"So, you don't recommend a number?"

"Oh, we do …" She smiled ruefully. "And Huron will bring that to the table. But the final numbers are out of our hands."

"Good to know," Rebecca replied, figures already swimming in her head.

———

"We can't take less than a twenty-five-times return."

Louise snorted in derision. "Exactly what world are you living in, Arun? No one is going to pay that."

"You don't know that. They want to buy Branches, so they should be willing to pay."

"Have you ever sold a company, Arun? Do you have any experience outside of a quick internet search?"

There was frenetic energy in the boardroom that Rebecca didn't quite know how to harness. They had been meeting for twenty minutes so far … and had made zero headway. Arun had been petulant and demanding the moon. Michael had been excited and ready to make a deal at any price. The rest of the board was present but so far hadn't contributed much more than "money." Louise was the pragmatic one of the bunch, but what she was saying was coming across as confrontational and condescending.

Rebecca wanted to shake them all.

Each one of the investors stood to make a profit off her team's hard work and their willingness to back her. But mostly her hard work, her ideas, her risking everything to keep it going.

They were not going to scupper this opportunity with greed, or over eagerness, or whatever the heck was going on with Louise.

She wouldn't allow it, if she could stop it at all.

"Whatever number we come to, it needs to have methodology behind it," Rebecca cut through the bickering. "Huron isn't going to pay an arbitrary number because the board wants to fund a private yacht." She pointedly looked at Arun, who huffed and folded his arms.

"Huron is coming up with their number based on value. We have to justify the value we see. So, if I can draw your attention to the summary page, there are four valuation methods we've hammered out and are open for discussion."

The packets had been prepared by Don and Rebecca. They had calculated three valuations based on different methods for justifying the value of a purchase, and a fourth that projected a "worst-case scenario" that would likely reflect Huron's opening number. The packets had been digitally sent to the board in preparation for this meeting, and apparently, the widespread in the numbers had set the cat among the pigeons.

Don cleared his throat. "Well, I think we should probably get the worst-case scenario out of the way. This is our projection of a lowball bid from Huron if they're going to start us at a very bare bones valuation. As everyone here knows, we have high expenses and a low software margin. In the very worst scenario, Huron could give us a number based on earnings revenue – basically a number based on our current earnings after the expenses are removed. As you can see, a three-times return on next to no earnings is unsurprisingly, next to nothing."

Rebecca stepped in smoothly, saying, "This worst-case scenario doesn't take into account the proprietary technology we've built – which is the whole reason they're interested in buying Branches. Our job here today is to figure out what that technology is worth to Huron and then come up with the rationale to back that up in."

Arun snorted. "It's worth whatever we can squeeze out of them."

"Ultimately, that's not far wrong. But they must go to their own board and get approval for the deal. The board is never going to approve the sale if the rationale is 'this is the number because we said so.' The final number has to be justifiable."

Arun flapped his hands in disgust, leaned back in his chair and folded his arms across his chest.

Louise pointed to the next number in the chart. "Not to pile on, but I don't think the times-revenue method is appropriate either. It just doesn't consider the value of the technology. Plus, Branches hasn't been open that long, so the revenues a year from now may be a completely different picture. The growth potential for Branches is exponential."

"I agree," Michael chimed in.

Rebecca was surprised and heartened to hear it. She had been worried that his excitement to make a deal would override good sense.

"I'm in complete agreement on that," Rebecca said. "The next number is where it gets interesting. Don, this one is a little complicated. Do you want to explain it?"

"Sure. So, this number is a build versus buy scenario for Huron to walk away from the deal and build the technology for themselves. This is looking at the number of heads we've hired, all our expenses, all our overhead, all the ways we've innovated on a bare bones budget, and then projecting what those same things would cost in California with expensive overhead costs and Huron's generous benefits package for every head hired. We've also baked in our pipeline and projected revenue. We know that Huron has a large list to fill the pipeline, but that doesn't negate the value of what we already have in progress."

"I'm sorry, can we go back?" Louise raised her hand like she was in school. "How do you know what their benefits package costs?"

"They were part of the disclosures. We had to do a comparison of benefits packages as part of the due diligence process. Every Branches employee that stays with Huron is going to get a bump in health care, 401k matches, more vacation time, paid gym membership, basically all the perks they could wish for."

"I wish someone paid for my gym membership," Michael grumbled.

"Well, gym memberships aside, we think it would take twice as long for them to get a product to market and cost them three times as much as it cost us to do the same." Rebecca tried to keep the boast out of her voice, but she knew it had crept in anyway. She was proud of what Branches had accomplished with few resources and an abundance of grit.

"This feels more like the right ballpark," Liz said. It was the first thing she'd said all meeting.

A few heads nodded in agreement.

"I agree, but it might be leaving money on the table. So, we've got one more number, and, full disclosure, we'll never be able to justify this purchase price. But this is what we think Huron will earn the first year they integrate Branches technology with their own products."

There was a low whistle from someone at the end of the table.

"I did a lot of marketplace research before I decided to go forward with building Branches. I did an equal amount when Huron approached us to talk. I think this is a fair guess at how much they stand to gain."

"That's Arun's yacht territory," Louise noted.

"I never said I wanted a yacht," Arun objected. Then he shrugged. "But a yacht would be nice."

"So, of all the options in front of us, we need a number for starting negotiations, a justification for that price, and a walkaway price." Rebecca glanced at Michael and a few others she was nervous about. "The walkaway price, for me, is the number where it stops making sense to sell. If it's too low, it'll be a better decision for Branches to continue building, raising money and crank out revenue down the line. So please keep in mind that by no means are we selling at any price."

There were a lot of nods around the room.

Rebecca felt her shoulders relax a bit. "Two more things before we dive deep into the numbers. First, I have a fiduciary responsibility to each shareholder in this meeting. That said, an individual shareholder's rate of return won't be calculated until there's an agreement in place with Huron. Until then, it's an unproductive use of time."

Arun started to get up as if to walk out in protest, and then winked and settled back down. It actually got a few chuckles, around the room, including from Rebecca.

Perhaps Arun isn't so bad after all.

"The second thing is that once we have our price range settled here today, I need you to give me the power to negotiate the deal. I don't want to come to the right number with Huron and then have to throw on the brakes to come back and get your approval. Too much time to think, and people can change their minds.

"Makes sense," Louise said, and Michael nodded.

Rebecca smiled. "Okay, so let's dive in."

Of all the names to pop up on her cell phone, she never expected to see Lindsey's ever again. But here she was, buzzing away on her desk. Rebecca hesitated to answer it. Their last conversations had been formal and clipped.

Here's your delivery of the final contract work and the reply I will review. And after years of working together, all communication had ceased.

Rebecca didn't realize until right this moment how relieved she had been for the relationship to end. And now, with anxiety roiling her belly, she decided not to answer the call. Whatever Lindsey wanted, voicemail would do.

Rebecca dove back into her review of the Branches marketing budget and didn't resurface for several hours. When she did, she was surprised all over again to see a voicemail from Lindsey. It was amazing what visceral reaction she had to the woman's name.

"Hi, Rebecca, long time no talk. I hear that Branches is doing well and starting to get some traction in the marketplace. Who would have thought? When you were calling me begging me to invest, I thought you were going to go under for sure. You should be super proud of all you've accomplished. And now that you've achieved some stability, I do believe I could invest in Branches. I also have a friend who is interested in jumping in too. Send your package my way, it would be $25,000 each, right? Thanks. Talk soon!"

Well crap, Rebecca thought. *Passive aggressiveness aside, what is 50,000 dollars worth to me?*

On the one hand, if the company sold, 50,000 dollars wouldn't move the needle at all. Branches would have all the resources it would need to expand and compete in the marketplace.

But if it didn't sell? That $50,000 dollars could be put to use. She could invest in more marketing, or conferences, or a million other things that could make the difference between being a minor player and a huge success.

No, she couldn't just ignore the opportunity. The deal to sell Huron was by no means a sure thing. But what really bothered her was the timing.

Lindsey didn't take risks.

On a hunch, Rebecca called Lindsey back.

She answered on the second ring. "Well, aren't you an eager beaver!"

"Hello, Lindsey, how are you?"

"Oh fine, just got back from vacation. Have you ever been to Aruba? The beaches are just magical."

Rebecca rolled her eyes and made small talk about beach vacations before coming to the point of the call. "So, I have to admit that your voicemail took me by surprise."

"Why? You called me plenty of times about investing."

"Yes, I did. And you weren't interested, which is why I stopped calling. Don't get me wrong, its validating for you to reach out and offer to invest, I just don't understand what changed."

"Oh, well, a friend of mine was admiring your company and how it was progressing. It made me rethink the opportunity. Since things are going well now, it seems like a safer investment."

"And your friend is interested in investing too?"

Lindsey made a noise that Rebecca took as a yes. "That's new. Nice, but new. Usually, I have to go chasing people down. What is his name? How do you know him?"

"Oh, he's just someone I went to school with. You wouldn't know him."

Rebecca waited.

"Harry Stephens"

Rebecca didn't know the first name, but the last name was very familiar. This was going to get awkward.

"Oh, I have met him," Rebecca bluffed. "It was years ago, but Harry probably doesn't remember. It was at Michael's birthday party."

"Oh, really? He didn't mention it."

"I'm not surprised. Do you know exactly what Harry likes about Branches?

It sounds like he has a persuasive argument that I should be using."

"Um. It wasn't anything in particular, it was the fact that he already knew about your little company and thought it was a buy."

Sure, Rebecca thought. *And the fact that his father is sitting on my board of directors has nothing to do with it.*

"Well, I can certainly send you the current prospectus on the company, Lindsey. There is, however, a caveat that investors need to stay invested for the duration. They can't dip a toe in and then sell their position. Is that something that you'd be willing to commit to?"

There was a pause on the line. "How long does duration mean?"

"Traditionally, the duration is until a change of control happens. Either the sale of the company, or an IPO ... or the whole thing crashes and burns."

"Well, that's something I'd have to consider."

"Okay, well think about it, take a look at the paperwork and let me know."

When Lindsey rang off a few minutes later, Rebecca immediately called Michael.

"Rebecca! How are you?"

"Well, I'm calling because I've got a weird situation going on over here."

Rebecca quickly recapped her call with Lindsey. She carefully didn't accuse Michael of insider trading, but she also pointedly didn't let him off the hook either. When she was done, there was a pause. "Michael, are you still there?"

"I'm so sorry," Michael sounded shaken. "We had Harry and his wife over for dinner last week. I mentioned that I had been busy advising a company that was close to selling. But I swear I didn't mention Branches by name."

Rebecca considered. He might be telling the truth. "Well, he figured it out. Can you reach out to him and get him to stop talking?"

"Absolutely. I have no idea how he knows ... oh."

"What?"

"He took a call in my home office. The paperwork must have been on the desk. Rebecca, I'm so sorry. I don't know what to say."

Rebecca didn't know what to say either. She didn't want to say anything that would sound like it was okay, because it really wasn't. There were NDAs for a reason and breaking them could have huge consequences.

The call ended a few minutes later after Michael reassured her that he would speak to Harry. Rebecca rubbed her temples at her desk. She liked Michael. But she wasn't sure she'd be able to trust him again. How would it look to Huron if she suddenly replaced a board member? Did she have that power? And what would happen if Huron found out about the breech?

Chapter Twenty-Two

---◆---

CALIFORNIA AGAIN. EVERY TIME SHE came out here it seemed all she saw of the Bay Area was the view from the freeway. One day, she mused, she'd like to come back and drink wine on the beach. Maybe once all the acquisition stuff was over with.

Rodney frowned at the grey sky. "I thought it was always sunny in California."

"Propaganda," the driver said. "It's only sunny in the winter around here."

"I knew it." Rodney folded his arms smugly and sat back in his seat.

Rodney was her newly minted Chief Technology Officer representing Branches at the negotiating table. Rebecca hadn't intended to have a CTO, but as the time to close the deal approached, it was obvious that Huron would want an expert to talk through the intricacies of the technology, and there was no one more qualified than Rodney. And Rodney had needed a title to back up that expertise. She had no extra money to pay him for the new role, but if the deal closed, she'd make sure he was taken care of.

Rodney was seemingly pleased by this, but also insisted that she "dub him" as CTO, like a knight.

So, in one of the more surreal moments of her life, a man wearing a novelty t- shirt that said: "Back in my day, we had nine planets" knelt on her office floor, and she knighted him with a dry erase pen. He had beamed.

She truly hoped that he had taken her request to wear something appropriate to the big meeting tomorrow seriously. Because right now, he was wearing a cardigan from a fictional laboratory and a t-shirt that said: "I paused my game to be here."

Rebecca tapped her nails against her phone creating a patter. Rodney glanced at it, but wisely didn't say anything. She knew she was a nervous wreck, and her constant nail tapping was wearing on him. She also couldn't stop herself.

Is it really worth it to leave Fritz, her freaking lawyer, at home?

Yes. It's too expensive to pay his flight, hotel, meals, and hourly fee.

No. If the deal falls apart, then no one gets paid anything.

Yes. He could help me negotiate a number.

No. The numbers are the numbers, if I can't do it, why can he?

She couldn't make the thoughts stop chasing themselves around her head.

"So," Rodney interrupted her circular thoughts, "tomorrow, do you know what the game plan is?"

"What do you mean?"

"I mean, are we all sitting around the table talking turkey? Or are they doing a divide and conquer thing?"

Rebecca paused, thinking. "Aw, crap."

"What?"

"They're going to divide and conquer. Why didn't I think of that? I should have brought Fritz."

"What?" Rodney sounded offended.

"No, not instead of you. You're absolutely the right person to have here. I just should have brought Fritz, too."

"Why?"

"Because when they low ball me, and I need to slow things down, I can't say, I need to speak to my lawyer in the hall. Because he isn't here. I'm an idiot."

"Can't you just call him? Step into the hall and pick up the phone."

"It's not the same. If they can't see the other person, they'll draw the conclusion that I'm not in charge of my own company. That I'm getting instructions from other people. And if I'm not in charge of my own company, the value of the company will erode."

"Well, can you say you need to talk to me?"

"Maybe," Rebecca said, but shook her head. She knew in her heart that wouldn't work. Rodney needed to slay his meeting, not play second fiddle in hers. She appreciated him trying to help though. "What I need … is a little bit of theater."

"What does that mean?"

"I'm not sure." A memory was niggling at the back of her head. "When I was in college, I went with a friend to buy a new car. And halfway through the negotiations, she said, hang on, I need to talk to my grandmother, and she proceeded to pull a full- fledged Ouija board out of her backpack. She set it up and her 'grandmother' said no. It was hilarious. The sales guy would get up and go talk to the manager to get a counteroffer, and my friend would then ask 'grandma' whether she should take it."

"Your friend is hilarious. Did she get the car?"

"Yeah. Grandma told her to get up and leave. They came down in price, and she drove home in a brand-new car." Rebecca chuckled at the memory. "It's too bad I'd be thrown out as a lunatic if I brought a Ouija board to the boardroom."

"Hang on," Rodney said with a mischievous grin. "How do you feel about Chinese for dinner?"

Rebecca's heart skipped a little and then she took a deep breath and said hello to Raymond Gomez, the CEO of Huron.

This is it. The big league.

Raymond's hand was dry and warm when he shook her hand, and she hoped her hands weren't noticeably sweaty in comparison.

He shook hands with Rodney next, and Rebecca paused to admire the version of Rodney that had shown up here today. He had abandoned his graphic t-shirts and tennis shoes. He had paired a sharp blazer with a cream button up, no tie, and wing-tip shoes. And somehow, he had known to dress it all down with a pair of designer jeans that looked like they were bought at the same store as every other executive in the room. He'd tamed his hair with a little bit of gel, and just like that, he seamlessly was "one of them." Rebecca felt confident that he was going to nail his portion of the meetings.

In short order, Rodney was swept away to an adjoining meeting room and Raymond, Calvin, and Alfred were settled at an executive board room. Looking across the table at the three men, Rebecca regretted again that she was solo on her side of the table. She should have forked out the money to have Fritz here.

It was too late now.

When the small talk faded, Raymond cleared his throat and Rebecca fought the urge to lean forward in her seat. *Calm. Relaxed. Confident.* She schooled herself to smile expectantly.

"Well, I do have to say that Branches seems like a good fit for Huron. We're hoping to finalize a number today and tell the lawyers to draw up the final paperwork."

Rebecca smiled and nodded. "I do think that Huron and Branches make sense together. Our proprietary technology will fit seamlessly within your product packages. When a solution like ours already exists, it just makes sense to acquire rather than build it. On top of which, I appreciate that you're offering Branches a chance to continue its mission rather than to just buy us to eliminate competition. We've been approached for those kinds of deals and declined them."

Raymond nodded. "I can tell that your employees are important to you. It comes through in the benefits and compensation packages. You take care of your employees."

"And I need to take care of my investors too."

Raymond shrugged and tilted back in his executive chair. "Investors always want as much as they can get and not a penny less."

A month ago, their opening number had been predictably low. Not the worst-case scenario, but not too far from it either. The negotiations had progressed, and they had each budged towards the middle, but the gap was still wide. The whole point of being here today was to come to final terms, and her "walk away" dollar amount was uncomfortably close to the current number. She had some latitude to wiggle, but not much.

"Don't we all?" Rebecca arched a wry eyebrow. "So, let's talk numbers."

Raymond's opening number was basically a recap of Calvin's last offer. She noted that and recapped her previous number to Calvin, with the corresponding rationale. Having established a starting ground, the negotiations began in earnest.

"I understand that you have a certain amount of sunk costs here. You've leveraged your personal assets to get this far, and without Huron, it will be years before you're able to recoup those investments. It would make sense to sell."

Rebecca wondered if he knew exactly how dire her personal financial situation was or if he was just taking a stab in the dark. The average entrepreneur likely mortgaged the house exactly as she had done.

Rebecca gave him the barest of shrugs. "My personal financial picture looks brighter every day. It would be a shame to sell Branches short when Huron stands to make a hundred million in the first two years after acquiring it. "

You're not the only one who does their research.

"Touché, though our projections are a bit more conservative than that."

"Naturally."

"Well, how about ..." and he named a number slightly higher than his last bid, but significantly below her walk-away price.

Rebecca's eyes flicked to the ceiling for a moment, then she mentally shrugged. *What the heck.* It worked, or she went home with exactly what she had when she arrived. So, she pushed back from the table a bit and pulled her purse out. "I don't know, I don't think that's going to be a good deal for Branches, but let's see what the universe has to say." She plucked a fortune cookie from inside her purse and held it up for the table to see. "What do you think?"

Calvin gave Raymond an amused glance. There was something in it that seemed a bit more than "hey this lady is crazy." That was encouraging.

She cracked her purse open, creating a small avalanche of crumbs. *Darn it.* She hadn't thought about that.

The white paper was peeking out from rubble, and she plucked it out. She had no idea what it would say. If it said, "Recognize success in the moment," would she immediately have to fold? She read it silently and then grinned.

"Patience is your ally at the moment. Don't worry!" Rebecca tried not to grin as she passed the fortune across the table. "Oh, it looks like there's some lucky numbers on the back, but since they start with zero, let's not use that as our point of reference."

"You are kidding. Where did you get these? Did you have them special made?" Raymond sounded genuinely delighted. He took the slip of paper and flipped it over, looking at the numbers. "No, definitely not special made or you would have had a much better number there."

"Well, maybe this one will have a better suggestion on the number," Rebecca said, and she fished a second cookie from her purse.

"No!" Raymond laughed. He turned to Calvin. "Did you tell her? How did she know?"

Calvin was grinning but he shook his head. "No, it wasn't me."

Rebecca paused between cracking the cookie and reading the latest fortune. "Know what?"

"Seriously, how much research did you do?"

"On you? Just the basic website, LinkedIn stuff. Why?"

He pointed to the fortune. "What did that one say?"

"It's useless, 'The real kindness comes from within you.' Ah, but the lucky numbers are much more in my favor. Oh, and a handy website to go gamble on. That can't be legal, can it?"

"For real?" Raymond was grinning like someone who knew someone was playing a prank on him, but he wasn't quite sure who.

"Real," Rebecca confirmed.

"Come here." And to her utter shock, Raymond stood up and beckoned her out of the room.

"This is absolutely wild," he commented as he ushered her into his office.

And there, in an ornate glass bowl, was a plethora of fortune cookies arranged just so. "I took this job five years ago on the advice of a fortune cookie."

"You're kidding." Rebecca laughed.

"Whenever I feel unsure of the right path, I pull one out. Sometimes I take the advice, sometimes I don't. But I've got a whole drawer of fortunes." And with a flourish, he slid out a drawer to reveal a heap of crinkled fortunes.

"You've got to be kidding," Rebecca repeated.

"You really didn't know? You don't have some corporate spy agency doing deep cover work? I'm not going to open up the next fortune cookie and have it say: 'Buy Branches at twice their asking price', am I?"

"Well, that would be a neat trick, wouldn't it? You should open one just to be sure."

He gave her a sideways glance before picking a cookie randomly and snapping it in one quick motion. "'The best way to get rid of an enemy is to make a friend.' Well, that's gotta be a sign, right? I don't think you're my enemy, but we're definitely going to be friends." He beamed at her.

"I genuinely just had Chinese for dinner last night."

"The universe works in mysterious ways. Come on." He put the delicate glass bowl under his arm and started guiding the way back to the conference room. "Let's see what else the universe has to say. And when all is said and done, the deal gift is going to be a fortune cookie."

Chapter Twenty-Three

FRITZ WAS GETTING PAID EXTRA for coming after hours. It had been two months since Rebecca had shaken hands over the deal and the paperwork was roughly a hand span off the desk. She was willing to pay her lawyer to come on a Friday night, because if she waited until Monday, she was certain some accountant or lawyer in California would decide they needed one more additional clause, invoice, or pint of blood.

Rebecca was getting it done tonight, if it took until midnight to initial every single page.

Fritz smiled as he flipped through to the next page and pointed out the very clear "sign here" sticker.

"Date this one."

Rebecca nodded and dutifully followed her signature with the date.

The lawyer's assistant took every page she marked with an initial or signature, scanned it, and placed it carefully in a pile to be overnighted to California.

"When will the wire transfer be initiated?" Rebecca asked. She knew she had asked it in a previous meeting, but she couldn't keep it in her brain. It was like a ghostly piece of information that evaporated as soon as she saw it.

"Likely Monday, when they get wet signatures and go through final approvals."

"And the funds will be in the account on Monday?"

Fritz gave a shrug. "If it's coming from the same bank, it might be available Tuesday. But it really depends on your bank. Some will hang onto it a couple days before making it available in your account. To make sure it's real and not going to be recalled."

Rebecca wrinkled her nose. Not because banks have to protect themselves, but because the uncertainty made it difficult to plan for. She needed to make sure the announcement to the rank-and-file employees was NOT the following Friday. They needed to see that things were stable by showing up to a normal workday, and not having a whole weekend to think too much about it. That would lead to anxiety and bad decision making. *People hate change that is completely out of their control.* She would need to create a list of to-dos, so when the money hit the account, she could roll things out quickly. "And how much is being held in escrow?"

Fritz consulted a paper. "Looks like twenty percent, for two years."

She knew that part. She was just nervous the leash would slip to three or four years. Two years was doable. It would put Tori into college, and she and Richard would be empty nesters.

How weird will that be? And at that point would I be retired?

Rebecca continued signing. She couldn't imagine herself as retired. She'd have to come up with something to do, or she'd go crazy. And she was definitely not going to bike her way through Vietnam. Rebecca's hand stopped, paused over the paperwork. *Is selling the company a mistake?* She was signing these papers, but did she really want to sell?

Fritz clearly noticed. "Is everything okay?"

"Yeah." Rebecca looked up, rolling her wrist. "Hand cramp."

He looked at her, knowingly. "Want to take a break?"

"No." Rebecca looked down, then looked back up. "Yes."

"Let's get some air."

"Okay."

They ended up at the rooftop bar overlooking downtown. The air was heavy compared to the sterile environment systems of the office. Rebecca took a deep breath. She hadn't realized that her heart had been racing until it started to slow. She deflated into a lounge seat in front of an unlit firepit. A few moments later, a waitress appeared with a chilled glass of white wine.

Fritz looked over at her speculatively.

"Whatever it is your feeling right now, it's normal."

"Am I that obvious?"

"No, it's just a natural thing. You've worked hard, you've built something from scratch. And now you're going to let it go."

"It's not the letting go part."

The silence drew out, contemplating.

"So many people helped me to get where I am right now. That networking group where we met. There were a ton of people there and people from previous jobs, and people I met along the way. People who didn't need to help, but they chose to. I almost feel like turning around and selling the company is ungrateful for their kindness and generosity, you know?"

"Gratitude is a strange thing," Fritz mused. "Did you know that in the

Sikh community, they serve community meals after services. And they don't want you to say thank you for the food. They just want you to accept the food with both hands. Taking it with only one hand is ungrateful. But when you're handed food and you deliberately accept it with both hands, nothing more needs to be said."

Rebecca felt her head rock back a bit at the concept. Had she been accepting the support she had been given with both hands?

"You're going to be getting a windfall of money soon, and so it will be really tempting to start giving gratitude in the form of payments. And for investors, what they want is money. It makes sense, and they'll take it with both hands, no questions asked. But for the random introduction at a networking event? The more appropriate gift would be an introduction in return. Otherwise, people are either uncomfortable or they begin to look at you as an ATM."

Rebecca gave her wine glass a swirl. "I don't know. It would be very simple to send a referral check to everyone who sent business my way. I feel like I need to make a gratitude list and make sure I find a way to thank every single person on it. But not thank them … How do you retroactively accept with both hands?"

Fritz shrugged. "When I figure it out, I'll let you know."

Rebecca went back to studying her wine glass. "What's going to happen next?" She subconsciously held a hand to her chest, trying to force all the fragmenting parts of herself to stay together. "I know what's going to happen next week. I've got a fairly good idea what is going to happen over the next two years. And then? Who will I be then? What will I do?"

"Ah," Fritz scratched absently at an eyebrow. "This is what I call, 'a new problem' problem. Your current problems are familiar. Making things, selling things, running a company, nothing there is surprising or beyond your ability to solve. You handle those all day, every day. And now you're going to put down all those known problems and step into a new life of independent wealth. The problems waiting in that life are completely different. It doesn't have the tactical, make sure you run payroll on time problems. It has the bigger, what do I do with my time, wealth, and privilege problems. These are questions most people don't get to confront, you know."

"I don't know why I didn't think about these things before."

Fritz shrugged and sipped his wine.

"I guess I was so caught up in selling the company, that I didn't think about what it would mean for me."

He nodded. "You wouldn't be the first."

"I don't know what to do."

"Well, try to frame it as choosing your problems. Do you want your current problems?"

Rebecca looked at downtown for a moment, watching the lights on the cars move up and down the streets. "I really don't. I want to put them down."

"Okay, Huron is willing to pay you a ridiculous sum of money to take those problems away. Do you want to let them?"

Rebecca couldn't help smiling. "Yes, I'm being paid to give away my problems." She pressed her palms to her eyes and groaned. "I can't believe I'm freaking out about this." She took her hands down and examined her palms. "And now I have smudgy eye make-up too."

After a quick inspection, Fritz replied, "Not too bad."

Rebecca gave a wan smile. "Okay, I think I'm ready. Let's go do this."

———

Rebecca had called the company-wide meeting for Thursday at 8 A.M. in a large conference room one floor down from the office. As excited as she was to share the news, she also was unsure how the team was going to react.

Would they be excited? She hoped so, but she also realized that change was scary and that her employees were people first. They were filing in one by one, helping themselves to the provided coffee and forming little clichés along project lines. They were universally giving her curious looks.

"Hey, Boss," a familiar voice murmured to her.

"Travis!" She beamed as she bear-hugged him. "I'm so glad you came."

"I wouldn't miss it for the world."

"Well, I'm glad you were game for this. I've got a stack of meetings prepped for you."

"Any softballs?"

"Mostly, but it's hard to predict."

He nodded.

"I think everyone is here," she said after a quick scan of the room.

Travis tipped her a wink. "Break a leg."

Rebecca took a long deep breath and let it out slowly. She guessed he was right, as this was a performance of sorts. *Break a leg, indeed.* "Hello, Team!" Rebecca was gratified to see all conversation stop as faces turned curiously her way. "I want to thank you all for coming in for this all-hands-on-deck meeting this morning. I know it's early, and I appreciate …" Rebecca paused for a moment as a latecomer scurried in, trying to pretend they had been there the whole time. Her voice was tinged with wry humor as she resumed, "That you all got here on time."

There were a couple half-hearted catcalls and chuckles, but mostly people just looked at her expectantly.

"I know there's been a bit of commotion around the office lately, and that you've noticed the closed-door meetings and late-night strategy sessions."

Some people nodded, while some looked utterly baffled that anything unusual had been happening at all.

"I've been really excited for a while to share the good news with you, and since it's now all official, I can finally share it with you: Branches has been purchased. As of today, you are employees of Huron."

"I knew it!" Bao said in accented English. She was almost on her toes with excitement.

Rebecca grinned at her. "Now I know there's going to be some questions but let me get the most important ones out of the way right now. Everyone in this room has a position with Huron, with a pay bump and an increase in benefits. No one is getting laid off or downsized."

"How much of a pay bump?" someone near the back asked.

She wasn't sure who it was, but it didn't really matter. "After this meeting, everyone is going to have a one-on-one meeting to go over your personal changes, as I don't think it's appropriate to talk about individual compensation in a group setting. You're welcome to discuss your compensation changes with your co-workers. But for me to disclose anyone's salary is a violation of privacy. Make sense?"

No one said yes.

Instead, there was another question from the back. "Will my health care change?"

"Yes. I think most of you will find that the health benefits are going to be greatly improved under Huron. A side-by-side comparison shows that deductibles and out of pocket maximums are going to be reduced. This is especially true for those of you on family plans. However, there will be a few of you that may need to switch primary care physicians if your doctor doesn't accept the new carrier."

"How will I know if I have to change?"

This was getting into the weeds, Rebecca realized, and realistically, this was always where the announcement was going to end up. *Might as well roll up my sleeves and dive in.* "There will be a transition coordinator from

Huron out next week to assist any employee who needs help navigating the change in insurance. Also, the Branches insurance will still be good for another thirty days, so there won't be a gap in health care coverage."

"What about my stock options?"

Rebecca smiled, at least there was no gray area on this one. "Great question. Everyone here, whether they started with us on day one, or last month, had a clause in their contract to cover this. In the event of Branches being acquired, all accumulated shares are fully vested and are paid out. I've a check here for every one of you, paying out the shares you earned over the course of your employment. They will be distributed to you in your one-on-one meetings, so please don't leave the office today without meeting with a strategy team member."

There was a murmur of excitement around the room at that. But the questions kept piling in. Were they going to get new titles? Promotions? Would they have to travel to a different office? Would there be a change in dress code? Would vacation days and sick days stay the same? Of all things, there was a cheer when she told them about the gym membership allowance. *Really? If that was such a perk, I should have implemented that one earlier.*

As the questions wound down, Bao raised her hand at the front of the group.

Rebecca nodded to her.

"What are you going to do? Are you leaving?"

Rebecca smiled. "I'm staying. I've signed a contract to stay with Branches under Huron for a minimum of two years. This will help with the transition and the integration of Branches into Huron's existing product line. And on that note, let me share with you the exciting places that Branches is about to go."

She outlined the overall future for the Branches product. The customer opportunities. The integrations. The innovations and the exciting freedom to grow with the company.

When Rebecca was done, there were more nods than frowns. That seemed like a good sign. She posted the schedule of one-on-one meetings and gave everyone permission to leave when their meeting was finished, if they want to go spend time with their families, but that it was business as usual tomorrow. A representative from Huron would be there tomorrow, and Rebecca would be at her desk bright and early, as usual.

Travis tipped Rebecca his trademark wink as he guided Bao into his temporary office. Bao was one of the employees that had been there since the beginning and had a sizable stock payout check waiting for her.

Don and Rodney were also pitching in on the meeting front. Rebecca saw them peel off with their first appointments. Rebecca hadn't booked herself for a first appointment so she could mix and mingle with the team and see how the announcement had been received. She was gratified by the handshakes and well-wishes. There were a few skeptics still left in the group, and she encouraged them to attend their one-on-one meeting. Each employee was allotted thirty minutes, so there was ample time to talk through all the individual repercussions of the transition. If they still had questions after the fact, they were welcome to come to her directly.

Most everyone seemed agreeable to that.

She didn't see Travis again until all the meetings were complete. Rebecca had wrapped up a session before him and left a message for him to meet her at the rooftop bar. Two Manhattan's were sweating on the bar when he arrived.

If she felt wrung out, he looked worse. "I've never worked so hard in my life to show someone that their good fortune was actually a good thing," he said as a way of greeting.

She laughed. "Truer words were never spoken." She nudged a glass his way. "Here."

He took a sip and sighed in satisfaction. "That's the ticket."

Rebecca led him to table away from the bar and lowered her voice a bit. "Seriously, though," Rebecca said, "how did it go?"

"Lots of questions. I felt like an answer vending machine. But nothing we hadn't discussed in advance. Other than individual doctor stuff, there wasn't much I couldn't handle."

"That's what I had. And I checked in with Don and Rodney – it was the same for them. One or two might still put in notice, but for the most part they seem okay ..." She hastily knocked on wood.

Travis obligingly knocked on wood too. "I wasn't too sure when you were facing the mob this morning."

"Yeah, I thought it was a little touch and go there for a moment too. I'm glad I did it first thing in the morning. Otherwise, the coffee would have had time to kick in."

Travis gave her a crack of a smile.

"I don't know if you're aware, but I owe you so much more than thanks for your help on this."

Travis gave a dismissive wave. "I'm just glad it worked out."

"Well, yeah, you're a good friend. But I remember what I promised you when we went to that Vegas conference." She had thought about this long and hard after her discussion with Fritz. There was two-handed gratitude, but there was also the financial gratitude. And Travis definitely deserved both.

Travis looked at her, clearly puzzled. "What did you promise?"

"You don't remember?"

"Did you promise to pay for the minibar?"

"Heck no. I couldn't afford to rub two peanut shells together on that trip. No, I told you that if you made me a millionaire, I'd put your new baby through college."

Travis went still. His eyes flicked over her face, clearly waiting to see if a punchline was about to drop. When it didn't, he licked his lips. "You, uh, don't—"

"Yes, I do." Rebecca reached into her purse and pulled out a white envelope. Inside was a check from her personal bank account. She handed it to him. "I couldn't have done this without you."

He didn't open the envelope. He was stuck just looking at her incredulously. "Thank you."

———

She'd had her Tesla for two years now, and she still struggled to find the right settings in the touch screen console.

"I got it," Richard said. "You pay attention to the road."

"Thanks."

The tennis tournament wouldn't take place until tomorrow, but Richard and Rebecca were driving up early to see Tori and take her out to dinner. It would be the first time they would see her since Tori left for college in late August, and Rebecca couldn't wait. How will she have changed? And to see Tori play in her first college tennis tournament? Rebecca couldn't be prouder.

Richard seemed to be thinking something different though. "So, your indentured servitude to Huron is up in t-minus thirty days. I know you really didn't want to talk about it. But it's coming up fast."

"It is," she agreed. "I know I've been hesitant to talk about it, but I can't wait to get away, honestly. The politics at big corporations are ridiculous. I feel like I have to wear a Teflon vest to deter backstabbers, and I never even wanted this job in the first place. The executive salary was nice for the transition period, but as soon as the final escrowed money gets released, I'm out."

"And then?"

She glanced over at him. "How do you feel about a vacation? I've had this dream forever of going to Napa. Trying all the wineries and gourmet food. Maybe starting a wine cellar?"

"We'd have to drink less or buy more to ever be able stock a wine cellar."

"They do have subscription boxes, you know. They mail you a case every quarter or something."

"Okay, we go spend some time getting fancy drunk. I'm game for that. But then what?"

Rebecca didn't need to look at Richard to know he was giving her a skeptical eyebrow.

"Any vacation we take, you have your laptop out on day three."

"Well, maybe I won't bring one this time. Maybe I'll bring a book."

Richard made a noise of derision. "And on day four, when you're finished with your book, you'll make me find an Apple store so you can buy a new laptop."

"Okay, okay. I'm ridiculous, and I know it. And yeah, I don't want to retire. I can't stop my brain from working. That's the woman you married, and if you don't know that by now, you never will."

"I know you." He picked up her hand and brushed her knuckles with a kiss. "I want you to be happy, on your terms, not glossy magazine fantasy island happy."

The miles spooled out under the car as she mulled it over. She stole another glance at him. "I started Branches because I wanted to build solutions. And the whole Branches thing was stressful and scary, and ultimately successful. I learned a lot from it."

"So, you're going to do it again?" Richard's face was a mix of shock and amusement. "Start another company?"

"I'm not sure what's next," she said with a shrug. "I've had a few ideas percolating for a while. There's a lot of problems in the world that could use solutions. But I don't necessarily have to create the solutions myself, you know? I could leverage my time and money in different ways. Branches was successful because of my network of people supporting me, the team I had around me, and the investors who funded me. I could find other companies with similar needs and pay it forward. Like invest in other up-and-coming companies, or even causes. I could consult with other entrepreneurs building companies, or volunteer for non-profits. I'm pretty sure that's what Louise is doing. I feel like I could take that path, and maybe she'd be interested in raising a fund of women investors with me. To invest in women founders?"

"Interesting – is there really a need for a woman only fund?

Rebecca cocked her head, "You have no idea, women get about 2.5 % of all angel and VC money invested yet we are more than 50% of the founders. I would love to go after that problem.".

Richard gave her a high five.

"I'm waiting for the 'but.'"

"But nothing. I want you to be happy, and I know from experience that using your brain makes you happy. I'd be a fool to tell you different."

She smiled his way. "You know I love you, right?"

"I do, but you could tell me again."

Rebecca grinned mischievously at her husband and let the miles roll on into the sunset.

Acknowledgments

I AM VERY GRATEFUL THAT the story of my first entrepreneurial journey is finally out of my head and in your hands.

Every step along my startup journey I reached out to old colleagues, friends, family and people I hardly knew, but whose contact information I did have. Soon realized I had quite a large network, community or tribe who had my back and were willing to lend a hand, a shoulder and a sounding board. Now, as I wrote this book, many of the same people showed up to cheer me on again. Who knew?

The bottom line is: I would not have this story to tell without all of them. We often talk about paying it forward, but for me this was forward, backwards and sideways. Their value was priceless, and I am forever grateful.

First and foremost is my friend and colleague, Jaqueline Kyle, who was with me for my first book and hopefully will be with me for my third and final book next year. Jaqueline has an amazing sense of humor, tolerates my crazy and has become a great friend. She is an author herself and she made this very hard job of book writing seem so much easier. She took all the rough drafts and outlines and my crazy notes & edits and together we created this book that you are now holding in your hands. She is like my daughter and my coach! She is amazing.

This book was nameless even after the first draft was complete; it was simply known as Robbie's Second Book. I brought back my naming team from my first book, and they will tell you this one was so much harder. (In truth, I was so much more difficult.) My longtime friend and colleague Ann Miller, her rock star creative husband Charlie Miller, my very best friend, my rock, my husband, Robert Dale, and so grateful that this time, my amazing sister and best friend, Ellen Garland. They put up with my flip charts and texts and endless emails and conversations until " Fed Up to Start Up" was finally on the cover. I cannot thank them enough for all their energy, creative ideas, and most of all, tolerance.

I also want to thank the thirty-two friends, colleagues and acquaintances who responded to my text asking them if they thought I could use the word Tribe in my title, or was it too polarizing or not? Some said yes but most said no, some sent other words to use, some sent some various definitions and articles on the word tribe. These wonderful people are part of my tribe and shared their time, expertise, and alternative options on the word Tribe for me. It might seem like a small thing, but it was surely big to me, and I am sending them all virtual hugs!

They are: Lora Allemeier, Suresh Balu, Neal Benefield, Tonya Dale, Jan Davis, Eva Doss, Mark Friedman, Vicki Gibbs, Ann Gonzalez, Lou Gonzalez, Paula Henderson, Nora Holley, Deborah Hylton, Jean Josephus, Karen Kilbourn, David Lapp, Beverly Malley, Tim McLoughlin, Margaret McNabb, Terry Moreno, Art Pappas, Sue Parry, Stephen Parry, Dave Pascua, Tammi Thornton, Jennifer Turnage, Leland Webb, Jeff Welch, Ed Whitehorn, Shante Williams, Suzanne Young, Craig Young.

Once again, my daughter, Tonya Dale was with me on this journey. She shared her thoughts and opinions, helped me sort out a few things, and of course was my sounding board for the book name and the cover image. Tonya has a great eye for detail. She is the very best daughter, and a really great friend – funny how that works. I love you very much.

My biggest thanks goes to my husband, who once again put up with the highs and lows of me doing a project with so much passion. I know it is such a crazy (and sometimes rough) ride. He is the love of my life, my very best friend. He brings me joy and laughter, is kind and generous, and who thankfully loves me.

And let me thank you reader. My hope is that you leave this book thinking about your network, your tribe, you community, your connections and recognizing how important they are to you and of course how important you can be to them.

It was a huge wake up call to me as I wrote the first draft of this book, reflecting on my start up journey, and realizing all the people who contributed to my success. I reached out to and they responded quickly and generously to offer whatever I was asking for... I had never really tried to measure their impact in any form, these were my "peeps" from 30 years ago to 30 days ago. Some I knew well and other just in passing but we had connected.

So who is in your network? Recognize and appreciate the value of your connections and your relationships. Go out and "network' at conferences and events. Drink bad wine and endure the incessant small talk. Informally meet people on an airplane, at a restaurant, in a meeting and the list goes on. Keep talking, building your network, finding your tribe! And always be ready to give back, pay it forward and not be so busy or self-absorbed to ignore reach outs to you from this amazing collection of connections.

So take a moment and think about who you met at what event that sticks out in your mind, not for the event but for the people you met – look at all your social media and bask in the awesomeness of these people who help make you who you are – as someone famous once said – "it takes a village" and it certainly does – Embrace it, nurture it and keep building it.

Thank you *for* Reading

★★★★★

Thank you for reading *Fed Up to Start Up*!
Please leave a review on Amazon, or your place of purchase!

CONNECT *with* **ME**

Visit ***RobbieHardy.Com*** and drop me a message!

www.robbiehardy.com